W0081568

HISTORY *of*
the Present

A JOURNAL OF CRITICAL HISTORY

Thomas Müntzer and the German Peasants' War at 500 Years

LOREN GOLDMAN AND MASSIMILIANO TOMBA, SPECIAL ISSUE EDITORS

Volume 15 ▪ Number 1 ▪ April 2025

Loren Goldman and Massimiliano Tomba

Introduction
Thomas Müntzer and the German Peasants' War at 500 Years

May 15, 1525: on the outskirts of a village in Thuringia, the combined forces of Duke George of Saxony and Landgrave Philip of Hessen confronted a hastily assembled popular army of eight thousand under the spiritual leadership of Thomas Müntzer, the radical Reformation's most strident voice. What came to be known as the Battle of Frankenhausen—the largest pitched engagement of the German Peasants' War—was hardly a battle at all: fifteen minutes after giving the peasants three hours to surrender, the princes ordered an artillery barrage. Thousands died on the spot and Müntzer escaped to town, only to be discovered disguised as a sickly old man in an attic bedroom. He was executed two weeks later, after interrogation under torture, supposedly having recanted the scandalous beliefs that challenged both Roman and Lutheran Christianity, his head impaled on a pike and his body left on public view for weeks, perhaps even months.

This year marks the five hundredth anniversary of Müntzer's death and the effective end of the German Peasants' War. The war itself, the largest European popular revolt before the French Revolution, was not a circumscribed event, but rather the culmination of a series of local uprisings that had convulsed German-speaking lands since the middle of the fifteenth century. In 1476 thousands revolted in the Tauber Valley, stirred by Hans Böhm, a visionary shepherd known as the Drummer of Niklashausen, whose call for the abolition of clerical and feudal privileges ended with his burning at the stake; from 1493 to 1517, in Alsace and Baden-Württemberg, a number of rebellions under the banner of the Bundschuh (tied shoe) movement were repeatedly and brutally suppressed; the same region experienced the "Poor Conrad" uprising of 1514, a conspiracy of several secret peasant

HISTORY of the PRESENT ▪ A Journal of Critical History ▪ 15:1 ▪ April 2025
DOI: 10.1215/21599785-11561465 © 2025 Duke University Press

leagues against their feudal lord, which was likewise decimated. Restiveness was not solely the province of the poor. Immediately presaging the greater Peasants' War that would soon break out, the Knights' Revolt of 1522–23—led by Franz von Sickingen and an army of lesser nobles whose power had been eroded by the consolidation of rule in the higher nobility and the Church—besieged Trier. After its failure, forced to flee to his own castle, Sickingen died of wounds suffered during its defense. While precise numbers are hard to come by, historians estimate that there were one hundred thousand peasant casualties by the end of the summer of 1525 (Miller 162). The war's subsequent denouement was also hardly conclusive, with significant uprisings continuing for years; a notable peasant rebellion, for example, soon followed in Tyrol, which protested against feudal oppression and economic hardship, drafting a more egalitarian constitution that was, however, never implemented.

Müntzer neither started nor led the German Peasants' War. As its most prominent thinker, however, he gave it a rigorous justification, and his writings not only embody its urgency and pathos but also offer insight into its participants' world. Much of Müntzer's own life remains shrouded in mystery, but its outlines are clear (see Goertz; Bräuer and Vogler; Drummond). Born into modest circumstances around 1490, he trained in philosophy and theology in the febrile years before the Reformation caught fire in 1517. Müntzer obtained his first significant clerical post on Luther's recommendation, yet his radicalism soon made an enemy out of his erstwhile patron. As Luther and his circle tacked ever more toward the magistrates, Müntzer aligned himself increasingly with the poor, whom he declared to be the true and only inheritors of Christ's mantle; it was they, he maintained, who would hasten the arrival of a New Jerusalem foreign to status and wealth. In a series of bitterly sardonic writings between 1523 and 1525, Müntzer railed against the Church and clergy, called for the end of feudal privileges, and endorsed the violent overthrow of the social order for the sake of "the common man." In addition to composing the first German church service, to which Luther's own vernacular liturgy was a palliative response, Müntzer printed salvos like "On Counterfeit Faith," "Interpretation of the Second Chapter of Daniel," and "Letter to the Miners" that circulated widely. Müntzer himself was constantly on the move, expelled from or having to flee nearly everywhere he arrived, from Zwickau to Allstedt to Mühlhausen and elsewhere. A talisman of popular discontent with the political order, he made common cause with incendiary lay preachers and was involved in several attempts to seize municipal power for the "elect." Luther ("Warning") accordingly attacked this "Satan of Allstedt" as "a false spirit and prophet, who goes around in sheep's clothing yet is secretly a rapacious wolf," and he urged the princes to "smite, slay, and stab, secretly or openly . . . a rebel . . . just as one must kill a mad dog" (Luther "Wider"). And killed they were: while the violent demise of Müntzer and his band at Frankenhausen did not spell the death of the radical Reformation, the legacy of which continued among Anabaptists, it signaled its end as a mass political movement and heralded the triumph of Luther's magisterial Reformation, which left the structure of earthly power largely untouched. The alternative, bottom-up model of political order that Müntzer represented retreated underground.

Müntzer's legacy is no less contested today than it was in his own time. Immediately after Müntzer's execution, Philipp Melanchthon lamented not having been permitted to interview him in captivity in order to better understand his theology. In the absence of such understanding, Luther's vituperation set the stage for Müntzer's reception, relegating him for centuries to the position of a dangerous fanatic. A slender 1608 Protestant volume published in Leiden entitled *Abominations of the Most Prominent Heretics*, for example, offers Müntzer's biography along with those of various Anabaptist leaders and even the Muslim prophet Muhammad "for the purpose of warning all pious Christians" against their blasphemies (see *Greuwel der vornahmsten Hauptketzeren*). In many quarters, similarly fearful and dismissive accounts persist to this day (see the discussion in Müller, *Mörder* 13–18).

The nineteenth-century rise of revolutionary turmoil in Germany and beyond brought renewed interest in the Peasants' War, and important works by liberals and radicals such as Wilhelm Zimmermann (1841–43), Johann Karl Seidemann (1842), and Friedrich Engels (1850) sympathetically reexamined Müntzer as an antipode to Luther, who was lionized at the time by conservatives and reactionaries as a font of German identity. Müntzer's works, long inaccessible, gradually began to appear in new editions, and Marxists in particular came to enlist him as a significant predecessor, with August Bebel (1876) and Karl Kautsky (1895) penning favorable influential treatments. By the early twentieth century, Müntzer was undeniably back in the historical imagination: in 1914 Hugo Ball (14) drew parallels between him and nineteenth-century Russian radicals in their common opposition to religious orthodoxy, while in 1921 Ernst Bloch's *Thomas Müntzer as Theologian of Revolution* appeared and Paul Gurk's play *Thomas Müntzer: A Tragedy* won the Kleist Prize, the Weimar Republic's highest literary award. Although Müntzer's appeal was mostly on the Left, National Socialists also sought to claim him for themselves as a *völkisch* leader against Marxist interpretations (Oberman 104). But in Weimar it was indeed among communists that Müntzer had the greatest purchase. In 1925, the four hundredth anniversary of his death, the Communist Party of Germany held a commemoration at the Frankenhausen site of Müntzer's last stand. Parallels were drawn to the deaths of communists in the reactionary Kapp Putsch of 1920, and a communist Reichstag deputy described the revolutionary German workers' movement as the continuation of Müntzer's struggle (Müller, "Reformator" 121).[1]

Müntzer subsequently became something of a patron saint in the new East Germany. The year 1953 saw the "Peasants' Battle Monument" renamed the "Thomas Müntzer Monument," with an inscription heralding him as a "revolutionary peasant leader against feudal oppression and exploitation, . . . who proclaimed the people's state in Mühlhausen in 1525" (Müller, "Zwanzig" 14). He even loomed large in cinema: one of the most lavish productions by DEFA, the East German film agency, was the 1956 color epic *Thomas Müntzer*, a response to the decidedly less impressive 1953 black-and-white American–West German film *Martin Luther*, which entirely ignores the Peasants' War. For Müntzer 1975 was a banner year; the 450th anniversary of his death saw commemorations throughout Germany and his image placed on the East German five mark note. In Bad Frankenhausen,[2] the painter Werner Tübke began a monumental socialist realist panorama, *Early Bourgeois Revolution in Germany*, which finally opened to the public in September 1989, ironically just six weeks before the fall of the Berlin Wall. While a thaw between East German Müntzer scholars and West German Luther scholars began in the late 1970s (Heise and Stache), even today Müntzer research remains in the shadow of this communist appropriation: many of his letters now reside in Moscow, having been given by the Saxon state government to Joseph Stalin as a seventieth birthday present in 1949, and transferred after his death in 1953 from his personal library to the Soviet state archives (Kobuch).

The contested history of the German Peasants' War mirrors the changing historiography of Müntzer's legacy. In 1839 Leopold von Ranke presented the war as a manifestation of mass irrationalism fortunately not integrated into the dominant tradition of modernity, celebrating the massacre of the peasants as the final end of a movement led by a fanatic "possessed by a savage demon up to his last hour" (355) that had threatened to overthrow German civilization and reshape the whole political structure of the world from below (see Blickle 7). Ranke's text was written when an entire social order was shattering and a new order was trying to rise, a change he looked on with despair; others welcomed the echo of Peasants' Wars in their present. After the 1848 German Revolution, for example, the liberal theologian Wilhelm Zimmermann brought out a revised edition of his 1841–43 sympathetic and influential *General History of the Great Peasants War* that put 1848 in a long emancipatory context: "Throughout the entire Middle Ages, from time to time, the peasantry rose up against aristocratic and ecclesiastical lords, partly to preserve their old, original freedom, partly to defend themselves against the arbitrariness that sought to forcibly increase the burdens on the unfree and turn serfs into slaves [*Leibeigenen*]. This struggle can be seen in many places across Europe" (Zimmermann 25). His introduction concludes with these words: "It's nice to please the present; but it is better to fulfill the future" (22). Zimmerman was well aware that the history of the past is the history of the present. There is something more, however: the critical historian ultimately aims at making room for the future.

In this spirit, Engels also wrote his seminal *The Peasant War in Germany*, after the defeat of the 1848 Revolution, and republished it with a new preface in 1874, after the defeat of the Paris Commune. Before the victors could wipe the slate clean, that tradition of struggle had to be revitalized to "remind the German people of the rough yet powerful and tenacious figures of the Great Peasant War" (Engels 16, translation modified). Engels does not write the history of the Peasants' War to pity the victims or give them a voice: it is still the historiography of the victorious, albeit highlighting the dark side of the same past. Engels's history is one of struggles, wars, and warriors, which he wanted to keep alive: it is the history of crushed attempts at liberation. For Engels, the Peasants' War, however "premature," should be considered part of the revolutionary tradition of the German proletariat. Reactivating this long-standing tradition was also a task Bloch set for himself in *Thomas Müntzer as Theologian of Revolution*, which, leaning on Engels, turns to this alternative vision of modernity in response to the failure of German council democracy during the revolution of 1919. The topicality of the parallel derives partially from the defeat, but primarily from the need to keep an alternative tradition to capitalist modernity alive.

Marxist historiography has emphasized social and economic changes in a framework in which the Peasants' War is often defined as an early bourgeois revolution, and Müntzer is depicted as a revolutionary ahead of his time. In contrast, a historian with a *völkish* orientation like Günther Franz presented the war as a clash between the community of self-governing structures of the peasantry and the centralizing tendencies of the new, modern territorial state (Franz). Peter Blickle, in a well-balanced examination of the different forces in the field, characterized the Peasants' War as the rebellion of the "common man" to change social relations and domination on the basis of the Gospel (Blickle). In short, like Müntzer, the Peasants' War was, is, and will be many things.

Moreover, the Peasants' War is not an exclusively German story. One could say that 1525 is the synecdoche of complex processes involved in the making of new legal, political, social, and economic structures—in other words, what is usually called the modern West. The popular uprisings challenged *both* the concentration of power in the monarchy and the privileges of the nobility. The uprisings opened a third legal and political possibility that is incompatible with both the royal and aristocratic poles of opposition. Historically, those who have ventured down this trajectory have paid a high price. The archives of the victors describe the insurgents as a "band of brigands" and "heretics" driven by "diabolical instinct" and "savage madness" (Cohn 99, 101). These are the terms used in the documents of the time. Historical inquiry would benefit from a comparative examination of these conflicts, by investigating these tensions from within, before the victorious won and the defeated were defeated.

The peasants were defeated. This is a fact. When Ranke (358) wrote that the movement of the Peasants' War was "now forever at an end," it was a prescription, not a description. The historicist claim to stick to the facts boils down to that. For Ranke, their defeat was a blessing because otherwise the Taborites would have "transformed the earth into a desert in the name of the Lord" (247). What happened in Tabor? Here, in the fifteenth-century Bohemian community inspired by the Hussite movement that had communal property and abolished the hierarchy between servants and masters, a mystical political experiment took shape, "not to overcome earthly difficulties in a new eudemonistic civilization, but rather for their derealization in the breakthrough of the Kingdom" (Bloch 64). In Tabor, Bloch observed, the fight was not for "better days, but for the end of all days" (64). This is what terrified the guards of the established order. For them, the end of their time and their days would coincide with the end of the world, with nihilism and a pitiless destruction. Nothing could be more wrong. The revolt was about ending a historical trajectory, that of private property and the nascent modern state, in order to make room for different trajectories. It was a war between a preestablished possible in the trajectory of progress and the irruption of a new time. This did not arise out of thin air. Nor was it the result of a dialectical reversal of destruction into creation. To move forward and create something truly new, one must orient oneself with a sense of direction rooted in the past. To return to Zimmermann, it is a matter of working on a "universal history of attempts at emancipation" (Zimmermann 7).

To investigate the significance of the Peasants' War and Müntzer five hundred years after their defeat, a different historiographical approach must be found. This is not a history of victims, but a history of attempts at emancipation that still need to be fulfilled, to be completed. As Walter Benjamin well understood, it is the incomplete past, not an uncertain future to be realized, that calls us to action. Nothing immobilizes action and blocks concrete possibilities as much as a present without history and a past turned into galleries of victims.

To remember Müntzer and the Peasants' War today means exploring the not-happened and the not-yet-explored. Politically, Müntzer asserted the power of the community over princes and the need for the direct presence of the people whenever judgment was made. He claimed the revocability of rulers against the tendency of princes to concentrate power in their own hands. He did not invent the revocability of rulers; he borrowed it from existing customs and reconfigured it. Similarly, he did not invent communism of goods, exemplified in the formula *omnia sunt communia* (all things are to be held in common). Against the trend toward the appropriation of common lands, Müntzer revived and combined existing customs and natural law with the tradition of the Taborites and Jan Hus. He revitalized the principle of common land existing in the mark system, protecting it in a theological shell.

Éric Vuillard comments on Müntzer's killing in these words: "His body will be dragged over the scaffold and thrown to the dogs. Youth is endless, the secret of our equality immortal, and solitude wonderful. Martyrdom is a trap for the oppressed." The texts gathered for this volume, five hundred years after the Peasants' War, aim to keep alive the call for equality and democracy, their history, and the everlasting hope of emancipation. ■

Loren Goldman is associate professor of political science at the University of Pennsylvania. He is the author of *The Principle of Political Hope* (2023), cotranslator of Ernst Bloch's *Avicenna and the Aristotelian Left* (2019), and is currently preparing a translation of Bloch's *Thomas Müntzer as Theologian of Revolution* (forthcoming).

Massimiliano Tomba is chair and professor in the History of Consciousness Department at the University of California, Santa Cruz. He has authored numerous books and articles on Kant, Hegel, the Left-Hegelians, Marx, and Benjamin. Among his publications are *Marx's Temporalities* (2013) and the Spitz Prize–winning book *Insurgent Universality: An Alternative Legacy of Modernity* (2019).

NOTES

1   Müller ("Reformator" 118–19) also describes a raging debate in 1921 over the representation of Müntzer and his comrade Heinrich Pfeiffer on Mühlhausen's emergency currency.

2   "Bad" was added to Frankenhausen's name in 1927 to advertise it as a spa town.

WORKS CITED

Ball, Hugo. *Flight Out of Time: A Dada Diary.* Edited by John Elderfield, translated by Ann Raimes. Berkeley: University of California Press, 1996.

Bebel, August. *Der deutsche Bauernkrieg, mit Berücksichtigung der hauptsächlichen sozialen Bewegungen des Mittelalters*. Braunschweig: Bracke, 1876.

Blickle, Peter. *The Revolution of 1525: The German Peasants' War from a New Perspective*. Translated by Thomas A. Brady Jr. and H. C. Erik Midelfort. Baltimore: Johns Hopkins University Press, 1981.

Bloch, Ernst. *Thomas Münzer als Theologe der Revolution*. Vol. 2 of *Thomas-Münzer-Gesamtausgabe*. 1921; repr., Frankfurt: Suhrkamp, 1969.

Bräuer, Siegried, and Günter Vogler. *Thomas Müntzer: Neu Ordnung machen in der Welt. Ein Biographie*. Munich: Gütersloher Verlagshaus, 2016.

Cohn, Samuel K. *Popular Protest in Late Medieval Europe: Italy, France, and Flanders: Selected Sources Translated and Annotated*. Manchester: Manchester University Press, 2004.

Drummond, Andrew. *The Dreadful History and Judgement of God on Thomas Müntzer: The Life and Times of an Early German Revolutionary*. London: Verso, 2024.

Engels, Friedrich. *The Peasant War in Germany*. In *1849-1851*, vol. 10 of *Karl Marx and Frederick Engels, Collected Works*, 397–482. 1850; New York: International Publishers, 1978.

Franz, Günther. *Der deutsche Bauernkrieg, 1525*. Berlin: Deutsche Buch-Gemeinschaft, 1926.

Goertz, Hans-Jürgen. *Thomas Müntzer: Revolutionär am Ende der Zeiten*. Munich: C. H. Beck, 2015.

Greuwel der vornahmsten Hauptketzeren: So wohl Widertauffer, als auch andern, welche viele menschen verfuhrt vnnd vms leben gebracht haben, so wol auss ihren eigen Schriffte, als auch andern glaubware Historien schreibers, neulich int licht auss gegeben, zu warnungen aller frommen Christen. Leyden: Heinrichen von Haestens, 1608.

Gurk, Paul. *Thomas Müntzer: Eine Tragödie*. Berlin: Oesterheld, 1922.

Heise, Joachim, and Christa Stache, eds. *Dialog über Luther und Müntzer: Zwanzig Expertengespräche zwischen kirchlichen und marxistischen Reformationshistorikern der DDR (1981–1990)*. In collaboration with von Johannes Gruhn. Berlin: Gesellschaft zur Förderung vergleichender Staat-Kirche-Forschung, 2011.

Kautsky, Karl. *Die Vorläufer des Neueren Sozialismus*. 4 vols. Stuttgart: J. H. W. Dietz, 1895.

Kobuch, Manfred. "Der beschwerliche Weg von Thomas Müntzers Briefwechsel aus Dresden nach Moskau." In *Archiv und Gedächtnis: Festschrift für Bodo Brachmann*, edited by Friedrich Beck, Eckart Henning, Joachim-Felix Leonhard, Susanna Paulukat, and Olaf B. Rader, 615–22. Potsdam: Verlag für Berlin-Brandenburg, 2005.

Luther, Martin. "Warning to the City of Mühlhausen." In *Quellen zu Thomas Müntzer*, edited by Helmar Junghans, 171–72. Vol. 3 of *Thomas-Müntzer-Ausgabe: Kritische Ausgabe*. Leipzig: Evangelische Verlagsanstalt, 2004.

Luther, Martin. "Wider die Mordischen und Reubischen Rotten der Bawren." Nuremburg: Jobst Gutknecht, 1525.

Miller, Douglas. *The German Peasants' War 1524-1526*. Warwick, UK: Helion, 2023.

Müller, Thomas T. *Mörder ohne Opfer: Die Reichstadt Mühlhausen und der Bauernkrieg in Thüringen*. Petersberg: Michael Imhof Verlag, 2021.

Müller, Thomas T. "Reformator, Erzteufel oder Protokommunist?: Thomas Müntzer und Mühlhausen." In *Historische Korrespondenzen: Festschrift für Dieter Stievermann zum 65. Geburtstag*, edited by Ulman Weiß und Jochen Vötsch, 115–40. Hamburg: Verlag Dr. Kovač, 2013.

Müller, Thomas T. "Zwanzig Jahre doppelte Vergangenheit: Zur Rezeption von Reformation und Bauernkrieg im geteilten Deutschland (1970–1990)." In *Sichtungen und Einblicke: Zur künstlerischen Rezeption von Reformation und Bauernkrieg im geteilten Deutschland*, edited by Rolf Luhn, Thomas T. Müller, and Jürgen Winter, 13–28. Petersberg: Mühlhäuser Museen, 2011.

Oberman, Heiko A. "The Gospel of Social Unrest: 450 Years after the So-Called 'German Peasants' War' of 1525." *Harvard Theological Review* 68, nos. 1–2 (1976): 103–29.

Ranke, Leopold von. *History of the Reformation in Germany*. Translated by Sarah Austin, edited by Robert A. Johnson. Vol. 3. 1839; New York: E. P. Dutton, 1905.

Seidemann, Johann Karl. *Thomas Müntzer: Eine Biographie, nach dem im Königlich Sächsischen Hauptstaatsarchiv zu Dresden vorhandenen Quellen bearbeitet*. Dresden: Arnoldsche Buchhandlung, 1842.

Zimmermann, Wilhelm. *Geschichte des großen Bauernkriegs, nach Urkunden und Augenzeugen*. Neue ganz umgearbeitete Auflage. Stuttgart: Rieger'sche Verlagsbuchhandlung, 1856.

Ernst Bloch

TRANSLATED BY LOREN GOLDMAN

Excerpts from *Thomas Müntzer as Theologian of Revolution*

We always want to only be with ourselves.

So even here we are by no means looking backward. Rather, we mix our-selves in vividly. And the others also return transformed in it, the dead come back, their actions want to happen again with us. Müntzer broke off most abruptly and yet he wanted the furthest. The person actively considering him thus has the present and the unconditioned within it more contained, more synoptic than all-too fleeting experience does, yet it is just as undamp-ened. Müntzer above all is history in the fertile sense; he and his and every-thing in the past that is worth being recorded is there to oblige us, inspire us, and to support us ever more broadly in what is constantly intended for us.

■ ■ ■

At the very least, these pages aim to conceptualize such relations. Into the present and coming days they mix early movements, half-forgotten, of which we are only still dimly aware. Of course, this work, despite its empir-ical foundations, is self-evidently essentially one of philosophy of history and religion. Accordingly, not only our life, but also everything it embraces con-tinues to churn and thus does not remain defined within its own time or within history at all, but instead as a figure that bears witness to a field tran-scending history. As in E. T. A. Hoffmann's tale, Ritter Gluck returns again and again to his room to play *Armida* more passionately; and Herder not only speaks of Shakespeare, but Shakespeare also speaks of Herder, of *Sturm und Drang*, musicality, and Romanticism. Consequently, history cannot be

HISTORY of the PRESENT ■ A Journal of Critical History ■ 15:1 ■ April 2025
DOI: 10.1215/21599785-11561476 © 2025 Duke University Press

brought into being by memory alone; add to the categories of efficacy or the historical value relationships the lasting legacy, the final impact on self and everything, the most authentic "reprint," the productive schema of recollection [*Eingedenken*]: as undeceiving, essential conscience for all that has not occurred, what is eternally meant for us, the untrodden, yet which historico-philosophically is likely to be trodden within what has already occurred, in the meaningless-meaningful mixture, in the chaotic crisscrossing and paradoxical guiding sum of our fate. The dead return again, in new activities as well as in new contexts of meaning, and history that is grasped, placed under perpetually potent revolutionary concepts, driven to legend and thereby illuminated, becomes, in the richness of their bearing witness related to revolution and apocalypse, an inescapable function. History is in no way, as in Spengler, a decaying sequence of images, nor is it in any way, as in secularized Augustinianism, a stable epic of progress and providential economy of salvation, but rather a hard, dangerous journey, a suffering, a rambling, a confusion, a search for a hidden home, full of tragic failures, of scalding, bursting fissures and eruptions, forsaken promises, intermittently charged with the conscience of light. So much in history that ruled and that raised high complaints was in truth, as Sebastian Franck recognized: laughter, fable, and carnival play, if not the devil's work to the public, certainly so in the eyes of God; but the defeated, Thomas Müntzer and all that his perspective teaches us to say, already belong in themselves to the philosophy of history, or perhaps even transcend history altogether; a palimpsest superimposed with the outlines of the Peasants' War, with the reflections of a different world as its foundation. So, appear to us—for the state is the devil, but the freedom of the children of God is the substance—, illuminate us and affirm us the rebel in Christ, Thomas Müntzer.

■ ■ ■

That is where we are heading, leaving the dead behind.

Nothing keeps us any longer where the feast is finished; we leave, we dream ourselves over. The enormously increasing vital urge of this moment feeds itself from new sources, its unquestionability poses a secret, still hidden faith.

Even if strong forces move against it, the human being still pushes away from the ground and over. We strive to no longer feel our outer life, we step out of it, which is increasingly subject to the machine and to domination, to the ultimately unburdening domination of the inessential. And the very same force that created the machine and that with a change of will drives it toward socialism also poses that secret, still latent aspect in socialism that

Marx overlooked, had to overlook, if he sought to finally put an end to misery and chance, but which in Müntzer's Germany and in Russia unavoidably holds onto its revolutionary-religious hereditary memory. Certainly, however, the enemy remains visible, recently entrenched in the solid complex of industrial power, and still in militarism, but not only with its ideology in ruins; rather, it will also be easier and more rational to expel him from this, his last patriciate, than from the old, disconnected corporatist petit bourgeoisie and feudalism on which the revolutionary momentum of Baptism shattered. But now the economic-political world of power around us—so insidious and hostile to value, long so deceptively illuminated by "culture" as the insubstantial luxury atmosphere of the dominant class—has become broken, unstable, and without purpose for all who belonged to it and up until now ideologized what is. Indeed, it is finally charged with an *immanent* dynamism toward its abyss, toward the open constructive horizon for everything suppressed, betrayed since the time of the Peasant Wars and the Late Gothic era, for all the unconditionalities of the will to the universal.

Thus the course of the external world cannot block virtue much longer and delay what is right and well anticipated. Rather, the centrifugal force of the same liberating movement is creative here, slinging the effervescent human race away from the ground and into its true space, where the immense higher worlds of premonition and of conscience, the half of the kingdom, expand. The time is returning, the proletarian impetus from the West will bring it back, it will culminate in Germany and Russia: there the peoples feel the presence of a light that dissolves the darkest of shadows, which suddenly shifts that which was overlooked, the heavenly subterranean, into the glaring center, which finally elevates the secret of heresy into the most powerful public display, into the pole and predominant principle of society. The underground history of the revolution that has already begun in the upright gait still waits to be heard; but the Brothers of the Valley,[1] the Cathars, the Waldensian Albigensians, Abbot Joachim of Fiore, the Brothers of the Good Will, of the Common Life, of the Full Spirit, of the Free Spirit, Meister Eckhart, the Hussites, Müntzer and the Anabaptists, Sebastian Franck, the Illuminati, Rousseau and Kant's humanist mysticism, Wilhelm Weitling, Franz von Baader, Leo Tolstoy—they all unite, and the conscience of this enormous tradition is pounding again at the door to put an end to fear, the state, unbelief, and everything else in the establishment in which the human being does not come to the fore. Now the spark shines, biding time no longer, in accordance with the Bible's surest demand: we have no lasting place here, but we seek the one to come; a messianic disposition is preparing to dawn anew, familiar at last with journeying and the undeceiving power of homeward longing:

not toward the silence of the soil, of works that have become ossified, of false cathedrals, of annealed transcendence, with no more fresh sources, but instead toward the clearing of our own lived instant itself, toward the adequation of our wonder, our premonition, our persistent and deepest dream of bliss, truth, disenchantment of ourselves, of secret divinity and glory. The world would never be so dark *above us* if absolute storm, central light did not stand ever so immediately before us: by the same token, our beyond has already been named and heard, still hidden behind a thin, cracking wall; the innermost name, Princess Sabbath, not less superior to all the gods who abandoned us on earth with only the palliative of a sobbing miracle that bursts in furiously. The spirit of genuine utopia shines high above the rubble and shattered cultural spheres of this world, assured for the first time of its pole in the innermost Ophir, Atlantis, Orplid,[2] in the house of its manifestation as the absolute We. In this way, Marxism and the dream of the absolute thus unite in the end on the same path and strategy; as the power of the journey and the end of every environment in which the human was an oppressed, a despised, a missing being; as a rebuilding of the star of earth and the calling, creation, and compelling of the kingdom; with all chiliasts, Müntzer keeps calling us on this tempestuous pilgrimage. And not only new life is dawning in the old reality, but every excess has become open, the world and eternity lie open, the new world of warmth and of breakthrough, of the light that rushes broadly out of the inner human being; now must become the time of the kingdom, our spirit that never forsakes and never disappoints shines toward it. We have had enough world history, there was also enough, too much, far too much form, polis, work, illusion, cordoning off through culture: a different life, an irresistible life is openly stirring, the narrow background of the theater of history, the theater of the polis, the theater of culture is disappearing; soul, depth, a sky of our dreams that expands over everything, starry from ground to crown, shines in, the true firmaments unfurl themselves, and our path of destiny leads irresistibly to that secret symbol toward which the dark, searching, difficult earth has been moving since the beginning of time. ∎

ACKNOWLEDGMENTS

Excerpts from Ernst Bloch, *Thomas Müntzer as Theologian of Revolution*, Gesamtausgabe 2. Frankfurt: Suhrkamp, 1969, pp. 9–15, 227–29.

NOTES

1   A fictional millenarian sect in Gerhard Hauptmann's *Fool in Christ: Emmanuel Quint* (1910).

2   Ophir is a biblical lost city renowned for its gold; Orplid is a fictional island utopia invented by Eduard Mörike and Ludwig Bauer.

Massimiliano Tomba

1525
The Insurgent Theology of the German Peasants

ABSTRACT The Peasants' War occurred with a backdrop of numerous conflicts stemming from incompatible political, legal, and religious differences. The clash between Müntzer and Luther represents just one aspect of a larger conflict. The established legal system faced a crisis, with the nobility upholding traditional customs and privileges while princes and territorial rulers sought to consolidate power through a newly enforced legal framework. Peasants and ordinary people disrupted this dichotomy by traveling an alternative path rooted in "godly law" and the "Christian common good." Although violently suppressed and its proponents massacred, this alternative path remains an unfinished possibility within the Western theory and history of modernity.

KEYWORDS godly law, Twelve Articles, Peasants' War, Thomas Müntzer, Martin Luther, kairos

The Peasants' War as Theory and History

The Peasants' War of 1525 was the culmination of a series of peasant and urban uprisings that began in the late fifteenth century in what is now southwestern Germany. These uprisings were accompanied by numerous strikes in the major mining district. The battle of Frankenhausen in May 1525 is the most notorious, not because of the high number of casualties, but because the defeat of the Christian Alliance (Christliche Vereinigung), formed in March 1525, put an end to the peasants' military organization and their confederal model that had started in Baltringen. The revolutionary theologian Thomas Müntzer was taken prisoner in Frankenhausen and tortured before being executed on May 27. In the numerous battles of the Peasants' War, one hundred thousand peasants were killed in massacres and executions.

Once the insurgency had been suppressed, the princes continued to work on "post-rebellion measures to prevent renewed uprisings" (Sea 220). These measures included the "common patrol" of the territory, the disarming of

HISTORY of the PRESENT ▪ A Journal of Critical History ▪ 15:1 ▪ April 2025
DOI: 10.1215/21599785-11561487 © 2025 Duke University Press

peasants, and the institution of "special courts and commissions" (235–36). The princes also "strengthened their internal authority over towns and villages" and claimed "additional rights, jurisdictions, and even territories at the expense of their subjects" (239–40). Through a new tax system, the peasants were also made to pay the cost of their repression. These processes were instrumental in the formation of the political and legal system of the modern state.

At the same time, Martin Luther provided new theological categories to justify the princes' authority and the subjects' duty of obedience. The categories of the Reformation and the political categories of the nascent modern state were forged in these battles. Hence their reactive and polemical nature, which modern political philosophy has in various ways tried to sweeten. Hegel's philosophy bears traces of this when he celebrates the Reformation for making the principle of individual freedom the banner of the new world. On the opposite front were the defeated: "Customs and traditions lost their validity" (Hegel 362). The life of the state had to be built on new rational foundations; "law, property, ethical life, government, constitutions, etc., must be conformed to general principles, in order that they may accord with the concept of free will and be rational" (435). According to Hegel, the essence of the Reformation was "Man is in his very nature destined to be free" (436). Hegel elevated a specific conception of freedom and rationality to a universal principle for the foundation of law and the modern state. These were, in fact, devices for stabilizing the order that emerged victorious from the Peasants' War.

The outcome of the conflict not only decided between victors and defeated but also granted the former the privilege of writing the dominant historical narrative. Philosophy arranged new concepts to guard the field of possibilities opened by the conflict. In his philosophy of history, Hegel celebrates Luther by repressing the Peasants' War and the name of Müntzer. In Hegelian terms, what was defeated deserved to be defeated, as it did not conform to the rationality of the present, which is the necessary outcome of the past. In describing "how it really was," Leopold von Ranke's objective historiography condemns the "extremely dangerous fanaticism" ranging from the Taborites to Müntzer's rejection of the state and property. In Ranke's historiography, a reverse teleology celebrates the definitive end of the visionary changes in the social order that occurred under the leadership of a fanatical prophet (Ranke 358). This is how a reversed teleology works. Its virtue lies in justifying the present by selecting one specific past trajectory and building a normative continuity between past and present. Reversed teleology does not describe; it prescribes. It polices the past by banning what must be excluded from the acceptable present.

There is a reverse teleology in Günther Franz's comment that the "peasants' war cleared the way for the princes to abolish the old corporate state [*Ständestaat*] and build the modern absolute territorial state [*Territorialstaat*]" (Franz, *Der deutsche Bauernkrieg* 298). In Franz's *völkish* orientation the war is presented as a clash between the self-governing communities of the peasantry and the centralizing tendencies of the new, modern territorial state. However, for Franz, unlike for Hegel, the peasants would have done better to defend the ancient right within the old order instead of subverting it with radical principles of Christian equality. Teleology also operates in Marxist historiography in which the Peasants' War is regarded as a "premature attempt" to establish the bourgeois society of a later period (Engels 137). In this case, a predetermined future arranges the historical material into succeeding stages. Engels worked with a performative historiography to channel the political and social energy of the past and present into a socialist future to be realized.

If we free ourselves from any kind of teleological perspective, we can see that the 1525 Peasants' War offers a range of possibilities in which dominant modernity, whether characterized by a centralized territorial state or by modern capitalist private property relations, is just one of many potential trajectories within the conflict. Different historiographical approaches are possible based on the selection of these elements. My intention is to show the production of new legal and theological categories on both sides of the 1525 conflict. The Peasants' War must be considered based on the concrete possibilities that emerged during its making and the opposing parties' efforts to defend or destroy them. This conflict gave rise to the legal concepts of the nascent territorial state, the concept of exclusive property, and new theological categories that were capable of justifying unconditional individual obedience against the old *jus resistentiae*. These categories did not originate in the minds of theologians and philosophers. Instead, they emerged through a clash with the theology and practical legality of the peasantry. Their nature is predominantly reactive, and as such, they must be examined as polemical categories produced in the intensity of conflict. The trajectory that emerged victorious from this clash used armed violence to suppress the insurgents and used theoretical violence to weaponize concepts and categories in order to neutralize the concrete possibilities contained in different political and legal trajectories. The concepts of modernity, whether political, legal, or theological, took shape as weapons against other concepts. The magisterial Reformation, the Lutheran variant, was shaped not only in a clash with the papacy but also in the clash with the peasantry and with Müntzer's "full and future reformation" (Müntzer, *Interpretation* 244). The dominant Reformation was the culmination of a war machine against different visions and practices of life in common. Ernst Bloch observed that in Tabor, this fifteenth-century community inspired by the Hussite movement that had communal property and abolished the hierarchy between servants and masters, a mystical political experiment took shape, "not to overcome earthly difficulties in a new eudemonistic civilization, but rather for their derealization [*Entrealisierung*] in the breakthrough of Kingdom" (Bloch 85).

If the Peasants' War was characterized by antagonistic relations between local autonomy and centralized power, this tension must be juxtaposed with another tension that unfolds vertically and aims at something deeper and higher. The insurgents of 1525 attacked the introduction of new laws not simply in the name of old customs, but in the name of *just* customs. The old law/new law pairing is complicated by godly law and divine justice, which reactivates old customs by renewing them. The historical dimension of customs functions as a deep justification and the reference to godly law as a high authority. In other words, when princes and lords began to concentrate political power in their own hands, insurgents defended local forms of authority by referring to traditions, customs, and God. The irruption of this vertical dimension, rooted in the higher authority of God and in deeper historical strata of tradition, disrupts the quarrel between old and new laws and suspends existing authorities. The vertical opens the order to change, and instead of the opposition between old and new law, institutes the tension between customs and right customs, between law and right law. The *seculum* is suspended in the consciousness that "things cannot go on the way they have done," that everything will change (Ranke 337), and there is a need to create room for the "restoration of the order of God" (Bräuer and Vogler 297). The vertical gives way to the eschatological dimension evoked by Thomas Müntzer.

It is possible to see the Peasants' War as a hologram that shows us, from different angles, different histories and possibilities in action. In the following pages, the force field of 1525 is examined as a tension between old and new laws, as a tension between worldly and divine order, and as a tension between secular time and eschatological time.

Old and New Laws

The defining elements of the Peasants' War can be summarized as follows: population growth, agrarian crisis, production for the market, intensified exploitation of peasants, increased taxes, restriction of access to forests and water against the common traditional use of these resources. Also: the intensification of personal dependency relations, such as the restriction of freedom of movement and the prohibition of marriages between serfs of other lords, against traditional village self-jurisdiction. And again: the clash between legal systems and sources of authority. The conflict between old law, natural law, godly law, Roman law, and new law circumscribes the legal sphere of the force field.

"Law arises not from innovation but from custom": this is how the peasants expressed their reaction to legal change in the early sixteenth century (Blickle, *Revolution* 34). This statement cannot be understood through the superficial binary categories of innovation and conservation. The peasants' declaration was made in a specific battlefield in which a new legal system revived Roman law to dismantle the feudal system, the authority of the estates, customs, and traditions. It aimed to establish a new legal order based on individuals instead of estates, guilds, and corporations, on private property instead of common ownership, and on the concentration of state political power instead of its dispersion in a plurality of local communities.

Roman law was used and weaponized by legal scholars in this clash with old customs (Whitman 17; Günther; Stern). A document written during the 1514 rebellion of Armer Konrad in Württemberg illustrates this dynamic well. The rebellion was directed against learned lawyers and jurists who, with their legal innovations, had plagued the poor and caused "disruption and disarray among the agreements and other ancient customs and usages in our town and villages—much to the hurt and disadvantage of the common man" (Franz, *Quellen* 51). The peasants rose up to demand a general reorganization of territorial law. Otherwise, "towns and villages should be left to their wonted customs, laws and courts, as these have come down to us from ancient times, lawyers and doctors of jurisprudence notwithstanding" (51). The controversy was not yet against Roman law per se, but against jurists who used it against old customs. In fact, Roman law and the Justinian code were not incompatible with "ancient customs," which were generally considered binding law and were likened to statutes (Strauss 100; Stein 26–27). The clash was over how Roman law was being used. It was about its reinvention by legal humanists, who not only distinguished between local rights (*iura propria*) and common law (*ius commune*) but also fought for the affirmation of the latter against the "barbarism" of feudal law.

What happened in the German territory between the fifteenth and sixteenth centuries was a political use of Roman law as a tool for the demolition of the feudal system and the centralization of power by the "modern state based on territorial integrity, permanent institutions, a standing bureaucracy, and the resolute exercise of sovereign prerogatives" (Strauss 136). This use of Roman law was initially opposed both by part of the nobility in defense of their privileges and authority, and by reformers such as Luther and Philip Melanchthon. Numerous proverbs expressed this perspective: "Keep hold to the old," "Custom does more than experts' lore" (105). Although in different tones, Luther and Melanchthon held to *ius scripture* versus *ius commune* until the early 1520s, abandoning the former only in horror at the growing unrest of the Peasants' War of 1524–25 (Whitman 19). When the peasants attacked the new justice, Melanchthon began to appeal to the humanist Roman law against the peasants' legal demands. Legal humanists provided an arsenal of concepts such as *tumultus, seditio,* and *rebellion* to define the peasants' revolt as a "violation of the legal order" to be met with military force (Mayenburg 191–92). Refusal to pay taxes or provide compulsory services was also considered a violation of the legal system. The new legal system was taking shape. It sought to equate law with the will of the state, rather than preserving the agreement between law and justice. This new legal episteme took shape in the conflict. It operated as a war machine not only against the feudal system but also and mainly against any insurrection that tried to give a different meaning to justice, freedom, and equality. The new legal episteme transformed instances of political freedom into freedom of the *forum interno* and replaced egalitarian instances with universal submission to power. It neutralized the question of the justice of the worldly order by dividing it into legal procedures on the one hand and the private moral justice of the individual on the other. The war for the new legal order reached a pinnacle of theoretical formalization in the Hobbesian principle *authoritas, non veritas, facit legem* (Hobbes [Latin edition] 202). In the early sixteenth century, before Hobbes and Locke provided new theoretical weapons to legitimize the nascent modern state, different legal practices and democracy confronted each other. On German soil, different interpretations of Scripture were part of this battle. Examining the political and legal categories in these tensions is like examining volcanic magma before the molten rock takes on a particular form. The appeal to medieval traditions and institutions intensified friction with the new legal order and inevitably raised the social temperature.

What emerged in the sixteenth century was not just the defense of the old rights and customs against the legal experts (*iureconsulti*), who, as Ulrich von Hutten wrote in his *Praedones* (1521), "having usurped the nobility's place at the side of princes, govern unimpeded, growing richer by the year and plundering everything in sight" (Strauss 28). If the nobles evoked old customs to defend their privileges and authorities, other documents clarified the perspective of the "common man" in the battlefield: "Everybody cries 'old customs' nowadays! But we do not say only 'according to old custom.' We say 'according to *right* custom'" (Strauss 105). When peasants, artisans, and miners referred to old customs, they did not do so to freeze an existing order, but to renew it. It is crucial to recognize that *novum* does not yet constitute a concept opposed to the old; rather, it signifies the tension between *potestas ordinata* and *potestas absoluta*.

In the Middle Ages, the "formula 'Good Old Law' was the strongest expression of a legal mentality for which law and justice, Right and law were in the end the same. This reflected a mentality in which all laws, orders, decrees, commands, were considered valid only in the context of Right" (Brunner 118–19). The reference to a *just* order to be restored had a twofold origin. The first is pragmatic: many of their petitions could not be supported by documentary evidence that could give legal validity to a custom. In fact, it was difficult to prove the existence of a custom based on a long duration in the *past* in the absence of a *present* written document. The new legal and political order privileged not only written law but also and above all the authority of the princes and the temporality of the present over tradition and historical continuity. Hence the recourse to another authority, that of God and the sacred Scripture. This is the second dimension of the reference to justice.

In the medieval conception, God is not only just but also the source of law ("*Got ist recht und recht komt von Got*") (Schmidt 5). It follows that whoever broke the law sinned against God and against the divine order. It would be a mistake to interpret this legal context with modern categories. Indeed, at first glance, it would seem that coating the existing order with God's authority constitutes an expedient to armor it and neutralize the possibility of resistance or change. The opposite is true. The unjust king is not a king in the eyes of God. Rather, the term to be used is that of *tyrannus*, a "man using force without authority" (Kern 101). Precisely because the legal order derives its authority from God, the justice of the secular order must constantly refer to a higher authority and transcendent order. Since even the highest worldly authority can violate God's just order, resistance and war against the tyrant are ways of restoring justice. New laws may be introduced because of the specific needs of the moment, but the new laws do not erase the older law, which continues to exist. What may happen is that the old law is overshadowed by the new law, at least until the old law is restored. But this is not a return to the old law, for what must be restored is harmony and justice between the laws. Conflict itself, in the sense of *jus resistentiae*, must be seen as the practice, participation, and restoration of a higher just order. Since the order of divine justice is not immediately visible, the just must be continually sought, even through conflict.

It is only in modernity that this theological structure collapses and the authority of the ruler becomes absolute: "The omnipotent God became the omnipotent lawgiver" (Schmitt 36). One should not be fooled by this formula. The modern theory of absolutism did not arise from the medieval doctrine of the divine right but rather from Roman sources of law reinvented for the modern use of contract-based government theory (Kern 36). Modern political theology has displaced the dimension of transcendence in the people, this new sovereign subject that is visible only insofar as it is represented: a "multitude of men, are made One Person, when they are by one Person, represented. . . . For it is the unity of the representor, not the unity of the represented, that maketh the person one" (Hobbes 109). The theological core of the modern state is to make the invisible visible or, in other words, to make the absent present by re-presenting it. At this point, authority is the result of the procedure of authorization through the vote of individuals, and justice is neutralized in procedures: "But what is a good Law? By a Good Law, I mean not a Just Law: for no Law can be Unjust. The Law is made by the Sovereign Power, and all that is done by such Power, is warranted, and owned by every one of the people; and that which every man will have so, no man can say is unjust" (Hobbes 230). The sovereign is such because he acts in the name of the people, who *authorized* the representative through the voting procedure and should be considered the *author* of laws made in their name. It could be said that the medieval order of God, justice, law, and the state, in which the last operates as a function of laws and these respond to a higher order of justice, undergoes an inversion. The state takes precedence and makes and rescinds laws in the name of the sovereign people, justice is judicial procedure, and God is a private matter internal to the conscience of the individual.

While from the modern point of view the law is to be considered legitimate and to be obeyed either because it is enacted according to precise legislative procedures or because it is enacted in an emergency situation, in the Middle Ages the situation is more articulated. The authority of the law was its age, and this was considered an important quality. When a law was called old, it referred to its high quality, not to its age. It would be wrong to assume an immediate and unambiguous correspondence between the age of the law and its rightness. The age of a law or custom was no guarantee of its rightness: "A hundred years of wrong make not one hour of right" (Kern 150). The reference was not to old customs as old, but to *good* old customs and *good* old laws, customs that have had time to be tested and slowly improved. In the event of a conflict, "it was the duty of every lawful man, of those in authority as well as the common man, to restore good old law" (150). As Otto Brunner also pointed out, "Even the peasant could and did appeal to 'the old laws' [*das alte Recht*], 'God and Justice,' and if lordship turned a deaf ear, the peasant could only ask if that lordship itself was not contrary to the divine order of Right" (217). Old laws were recalled as just and old because they were referred to in a practical contestation of the moment. In this sense, the peasants referred to old laws as divine laws to restore the good order violated by the princes.

For sixteenth-century peasants, the reference to justice and God introduced a dynamic element into the understanding and enactment of the law. These are the terms of the conflict: on the one hand, the social forces that supported the new order maintained centralization and concentration at the summit of political power but disintegration of the authorities at the ground level. On the other, the peasants worked with and reconfigured an alternative practice of the law inspired by the preservation of a concord between the law, customs, and the principles of justice that governed the world. The proximity between law and godly law, between justice and divine justice, creates a tension that makes the earthly order open to change. It was this tension that raised the temperature at Mühlhausen. The armed violence of the princes, the legal violence of the jurists, and the theological violence of Luther combined to eliminate the concrete possibility of different legal systems, forms of possession, and confederative political institutions practiced by the peasants.

The Twelve Articles: Law and Godly Law

The second articulation of tension in the Peasants' War is well represented in the most famous of the many documents produced in the early sixteenth century: The *Twelve Articles of the Swabian Peasants*. In just two months, twenty editions and twenty-five thousand copies were printed. The articles circulated from Thuringia to Tyrol, from Alsace to Salzburg. Letterpress printing, introduced a few decades earlier, acted as a powerful means of disseminating texts and as a catalyst for new possibilities of democratization.

The articles were discussed at a peasants' assembly in the free imperial city of Memmingen and constituted the main document of the Memmingen Bundesordnung. This was an alternative peasants' confederation to the Swabian League, which was established in 1488 by Emperor Frederick III of Habsburg. The confederation was based on a network of peasant communities that served as both the institutional infrastructure of the insurgency and the practical realization of an alternative political and legal system. This system was created in response to both the medieval hierarchical organization and the increasing concentration of political power by the state.

The Twelve Articles did not come out of thin air. Many other articles were published in different parts of the German territory. In May 1524 the town of Forchheim published five articles that began with this statement: "All waters, birds, and animals should be common and free for hunting" (Franz, *Quellen* 315). The tone of the sixteen articles of the peasants in the Brigach Valley (November 18, 1524) was similar: "All wild animals, water, and birds should be free" (Baumann 97). The collection of all these articles constitutes an archive for the history of democracy and the practice of the commons, whose importance is not inferior to that of the Magna Carta for the affirmation of liberties. In fact, both the Magna Carta and the German articles do not list rights, but perpetuities that go "deep into human history" (Linebaugh 45).

The Twelve Articles were drafted between late February and March 1, 1525. Sebastian Lotzer, on behalf of twenty-seven villages and the Baltringen troop of seven thousand or more rebellious peasants north of Memmingen, reduced the list to twelve articles. Christoph Schappeler, a priest from Memmingen who was excommunicated in 1524, wrote the introduction, which is the theological justification for the articles. There are sixty biblical references in the margins of the articles. The articles have been read and interpreted in different ways: as a moderate text (Mayenburg 259); or as a manifesto defending common property, agrarian communism, and a form of rule based on participation and self-government (Scott and Scribner 252–57; Blickle, *Revolution* 25–57). Certainly, their publication raised the already high temperature of March 1525 even further. Luther and Melanchthon intervened to condemn not only the incipient revolt but also and especially its justification, that is, the political-theological armor and some of the principles contained in the articles.

Here is an outline of the Twelve Articles that aimed to restore a just order of things (Franz, *Quellen* 174–79; Scott and Scribner 252–57).

The preamble and concluding article 12 emphasize the consistency of the articles with Scripture and divine law. Article 1 gives the congregation the power to choose and dismiss the pastor, removing this power from other authorities. Article 2 requires the regulation of tithes in relation to the needs of the community and their collection by a member elected by the community. Its importance becomes evident when one considers Luther's reaction: "This is the same thing as deposing the rulers altogether" (Luther, *Ermahnung* 326). Article 3 abolishes serfdom. Articles 4 and 5, relating to customs that regulated hunting, fishing, and the cutting of wood, aim to regulate the use of common resources according to the principle of brotherhood. Similarly, article 10 aims to return to the community the pastures and arable land unjustly appropriated by the lords. Articles 6, 7, and 8 redefine the limits of labor service, the limits of the lords in relation to the labor of the peasants, and the right to receive just compensation for labor performed. Articles 9 and 11 place further limits on the lords' authority over inheritance taxes and criminal jurisdiction, which was increasingly exercised arbitrarily by judges under the new laws.

Melanchthon attacked each of the twelve articles as contrary to the law, to Roman law, to the superior authority of the lords, and to God. Both Luther and Melanchthon considered the articles anti-Christian because they called for disobedience and rebellion. Luther objected that even if the articles might be just according to the law of nature (*natürlich recht*), they went against Christian law (*Christlich recht*), which instead teaches obedience to authority, respect for the existing order, submission, and patience (Luther, *Ermahnung* 319). In controversy with the legality of the peasants, Luther introduced here a difference between Christian and natural law; where the latter, in the Middle Ages, was used to designate both good, old, historically established laws and an ideal order based on brotherly love (Sprandel).

The third article—"We Are Free and We Wish to Be Free"—opposes servitude because it goes against the principles of brotherhood and freedom taught in the Scriptures. This article provoked Luther's fury. It is useful to start from his fury, to better understand the incendiary nature of the article. Luther summarizes it as follows: "There shall be no serfs [*Leibeygene*], for Christ has set all free" (Luther, *Ermahnung* 326). Because it would abolish serfdom, the article would, according to Luther, "make all men equal." Luther raises both legal and theological objections. Writing as a theologian, Luther objected that Abraham and other patriarchs had slaves, and that Paul taught the servants obedience: in the worldly kingdom, inequality would constitute the order of things. From a legal standpoint, serfdom (*Leibeigenschaft*) was defined by personal dependency, with individuals being legally bound to a specific lord and territory. This bond corresponded to a form of ownership over the peasant's body (*Leib*) (Sabean 87–99). The concept of serfdom took on a more defined and intensified character as a result of the medieval agrarian crisis, the need to have sufficient labor to work the fields, and to limit the mobility of serfs (Blickle, *Revolution* 32–33; Buszello 110–11). Recent studies have pointed to a significant improvement in the status of the peasants in this period, particularly in terms of their right to leave the lord's territory (Sreenivasan). What matters is the reaction of the peasants. In general, rebellions take place when there is a glimmer of improvement, not when they are sinking into ever-worsening conditions. As early as the late fifteenth century, documents circulated denouncing the ownership of peasants' bodies. The peasants had their own sources and traditions, such as the *Schwabenspiegel*, the thirteenth-century legal code republished in 1473. The code explicitly states that God created man in his own image and likeness, and originally "people were all free. . . . In the old scripture we do not find that one man is the owner of another [*vinden wir niht, daß ein man des andern eigen ist*]" (Schmidt 5–6; Blickle, *Der Bauernkrieg* 63). Similarly, *Das Buch der hundert Kapitel*, written between 1498 and 1510, asserted the notion of common ancestry from Adam as opposed to notions of servitude and privilege (Franke 245).

But Luther denounced the insurgent tradition. Commenting on the Twelve Articles, he called the third article a robbery because it would justify the theft of the servant's body (*Leib*), which is the lord's property (Luther, *Ermahnung* 65). The relationship between mastery and serfdom was political and did not concern only feudal lords. Abbeys and monasteries could demand services, exact obedience, and punish subjects. This is especially important when one considers the peasants' demand, expressed in the first article, to have the power to choose, elect, and depose their pastor. What was at stake was a radical reconfiguration of power relations. Given the overlap between property and dominion, the abolition of serfdom must have appeared to the feudal lords, as well as to Luther, as an attempt to destroy the foundations of the existing order and, at the same time, to abolish dominion and government. Hence the peasants' caution, if such a subversive avowal can be called caution, when in the third article they state that they "will gladly obey" their "elected and appointed rulers," for these rulers, as good Christians, will release the peasants from serfdom. Abolition of serfdom, control of rulers, and the election and dismissal of pastors should be considered together because the abolition of serfdom was not based on individual civil rights, which were unthinkable in the legal context of the sixteenth century, but on a modification of power relations by appealing to a different tradition.

But Luther, in the famous incipit of his *On the Freedom of a Christian* (1520), wrote, "A Christian is a free lord of all things and is subject to no one. A Christian is a dutiful servant in all things and is subject to everyone" (Luther, *Von der Freiheit* 21). The Lutheran notion of "freedom" takes on its proper coloring when illuminated in the historical context of the *Bundschuh* uprisings against serfdom, ecclesiastic privileges, the prohibitions on hunting and fishing, and others, which began in 1493, when Luther was still a child (Blickle, "Bundschuh"; Laube; Rosenkranz). Luther's entire life was characterized by his fear of social instability caused by constant peasant rebellions. By distinguishing between internal and external man, Luther sought to preserve and encapsulate the Christian freedom of the individual within a context of obedience to the laws of worldly order and the authority of the princes. In the final pages of *On the Freedom of a Christian*, Luther referred to Romans 13 to urge Christians to obey worldly authority "even if tyrants act unjustly." Obedience does not harm the Christian, "as it is not contrary to God" (Luther, *Von der Freiheit* 37). The important thing was to contain Christian freedom by locating it in the consciousness of the individual, without changing the order of power relations. The modern concept of "freedom" emerged and functioned as a polemical concept to extinguish the fire of the peasant Reformation and neutralize its possible political consequences. Hence the dichotomization of freedom into internal and external, private and public.

Melanchthon further explores the point that inequalities, forms of possession, and legal systems, be they the "Saxon law or Roman law," do not affect the life of the Christian: spiritual freedom is to be kept separate from the worldly order (Melanchthon, "Gutachten" 184–85). By means of the dichotomy between earthly order and heavenly order, the tension between theology and politics was neutralized. This is the script that modernity will play out under the label of secularism. Religion is sucked into the inner forum of individual consciousness and politically neutralized. Political sovereignty is concentrated at the top of the state. The *societas civilis* is pulverized into individual atoms, equal in that they are all equally subject to the authority of the state. Freedom is circumscribed by the laws of the state, so that individual freedoms can coexist alongside one another.

In opposition to Luther and Melanchthon, the Twelve Articles presented and defended an alternative legal system and way of life by combining godly law and old law. The preamble to the articles presents the Gospel as their true foundation. The preamble defends the peasants against both the accusation of being "disobedient and rebellious" and the accusation of wanting to overthrow ecclesiastical and secular authority in the name of the Gospel. Indeed, the accusation is reversed: the peasants want "to hear the Gospel and live according to it" (Scott and Scribner 253). Because they want to obey the Gospel and live according to its righteous laws, the peasants cannot be considered disobedient. On the contrary, those who attack them must be considered disobedient and rebellious to the authority of the Gospel. This is not a rhetorical reversal. The issue of obedience is central. The clash is between legal systems, obligations, authorities: the authority of the princes, that of traditional customs, and that of God. A central role is played by the interpretation of Romans 13,[1] which Luther uses as a weapon against the peasants: "Let every soul be subjected to the higher authority with fear and reverence" (Luther, *Ermahnung* 303). The last two words are Luther's addition to the Pauline text. In *Against the Robbing and Murdering Hordes of Peasants*, Luther's reading of Romans 13 affirms obedience to governing authorities and condemns all forms of rebellion as "an outlaw to God and the emperor," and he invites everyone to "smite, slay, and stab, secretly or openly . . . a rebel. . . . just as one must kill a mad dog" (Luther, *Wider den Reubischen* 358).

Romans 13 does not appear in the preamble of the Twelve Articles, but it is mentioned in the third article to specify that the freedom claimed by the peasants is not "free license of the flesh," but a way of living in accordance with the authority of the Gospel and the commandments. Not only that. The Pauline passage is mentioned a second time to explain that the peasants are happy to obey an appointed authority who acts in a Christian manner, that is, an authority who does not treat the peasants as servants. The emphasis is on the lines following Romans 13. There is no reason to fear rulers if what is "right" (Romans 13:3–4) is being done, and this higher justice must be adhered to by rulers as well. Authority comes from God and deserves obedience only insofar as it conforms to what is right. Luther's interpretation is reversed. Thomas Müntzer had presented this alternative reading in several writings. In a letter to Count Ernst von Mansfeld, dated September 22, 1523, Müntzer had written that Romans 13 teaches to fear God alone, and when the princes want to be feared more than God, they take away the key to the knowledge of God from the people (*Collected Works* 67). Müntzer combines a mystical tradition in which the fear of God must make room for God to restore the inner order and the transformation of the outer order to restore the just order violated by the egoism of the princes. Divine fear becomes an engine of transformation. It produces an inner emptying and detachment from the world as a function of the true transformation of both the inner man and the outer world. Internal and external transformations are not temporally separated stages; rather, they constitute the dual aspects of Müntzer's full reformation.

Luther's Reformation was moving in an opposite direction. In texts written between 1520 and 1525, Luther elaborated the doctrine that separated the inner man from the outer man, the spiritual or divine government from the secular or human one. These texts must be read as a reply to the texts and documents of the peasants. If the peasants invoked godly law to challenge the relations of serfdom and obedience to unjust lords, the political theology of the dominant Reformation made it compatible with obedience and serfdom by internalizing Christian freedom. At the same time, the two kingdoms doctrine neutralized the appeal to Scripture as a source of authority for judging the actions of the princes. This one-to-one confrontation can be seen in Müntzer's *Schutzrede* (1524). Here Müntzer responds to Luther's writings on authority and answers the *Letter to the Princes of Saxony, Concerning the Rebellious Spirit* (1524), in which Luther had directly attacked him. The contrast between the two works is already apparent in the dedications. All the titles used by Luther to honor the princes are taken up polemically by Müntzer. However, Müntzer doesn't use these titles to honor other princes, but rather to honor Jesus Christ. The reference is to a different authority, superior to that of the princes. If Luther had given the sword to the princes, Müntzer put it back into the hands of the community. Since God has priority over rulers, if they do not act in a pious way, "the sword will be taken from them and will be given to the people," wrote Müntzer to Friedrich the Wise on October 4, 1523 (*Collected Works* 69, 142). In the *Schutzrede*, Müntzer reiterates that "the power of the sword as well as the key to release sins is in the hands of the whole community. . . . [P]rinces are not lords over the sword but servants of it" (*Vindication* 334). Müntzer's insurgent theology limited the power of the princes and reestablished justice as the constant criterion of their actions before the community and God.

Through the mediation of New and Old Testament texts, Müntzer draws democratic implications for changing the existing order: "The kingship and dominion . . . shall be given to the people" (Daniel 7:27). Since the princes prefer to be feared than to act justly, it is up to the community to create a just habitat in which it is finally possible to live as brothers. The principle of brotherhood, which is repeated in the articles, is also an inclusive political principle (Roper 61–62). It is not a private, modern, sentimental love of neighbor, but a highly inclusive idea and an active principle for transforming the world so that we can finally live as brothers. It is not the friend whom we have chosen to live with in community, but the other (ἕτερον) whom we have not chosen.[2] Practical brotherhood changes the world so that we can live alongside one another as brothers. It is not the expansion of modern sentimental love that changes the existing state of affairs. This love can be withdrawn by any individual at any time. Love for others and brotherhood are not guidelines for individual good moral consciousness, but principles for transforming the existing order so that we can live with and love those we have not chosen. In the context of Romans 13, where Paul speaks of love for others, all the pronouns used are in the plural. The reference is to community and collective experience. In the early modern age of Europe, it was not only the alternative between incompatible legal systems that was decided, but also a different relationship between individual and community anthropology. Indeed, the individualization of consciousness is a modern construction facilitated by the dominant Reformation.

Kairos. Es ist Zeit

The third level of articulation of the Peasants' War is theological and hence highly political. The preamble to the Twelve Articles concludes with a parallel between the peasants and the children of Israel in the hands of the Pharaoh. It reads that God will save the peasants today, just as he saved the children of Israel. And "he will save them soon" (Scott and Scribner 253). This sense of the shortening of time was common to the peasants and their insurgent theologian Thomas Müntzer. God sees the struggles of his elect, and he "is sure to shorten the days of his elect," wrote Müntzer in the *Exposé of False Faith*, paraphrasing Matthew 24:22 (*Testimony* 280). The days will be abbreviated (*verkürtzen*) (280). Müntzer had repeatedly condemned Luther's inaction. "It is time. Do not delay (*Es ist zeyt! Nolite tardare*)," he had written to Melanchthon on March 29, 1522 (*Thomas-Müntzer-Ausgabe*, 2: 127). This dispute over time is exquisitely theological-political. It concerns *kairos* and its political implications. *Kairos* is not simply the time of opportunity, a chance for decision and action, as it is often simplified. It is more complex, and it is no coincidence that there is no modern term to translate it properly. *Kairos* is the time in coexistence and in tension with *chronos*. This tension is between worldly time and that of the kingdom of God. From the tension between simultaneously present times, that is, *chronos* and the eternity of the kingdom of God, there follows the political problem of the placement of *kairos* and the temporality of the kingdom of God. In the Greek translation of the Old Testament, the difference is illustrated in these terms: "There is a time [χρόνος] for everything, and a time [καιρὸς] for every activity under the heavens" (Ecclesiastes 3:1). All events occur within *chronos*, but it is their qualitative differences that render an event decisive for the sense of past, present, and future. This qualitative difference requires orientation and a precise understanding of the current situation to determine the appropriate moment for intervention and its quality. Kairotic intervention ensures that the succeeding moment is not the continuation of the previous one. The tension between time (*chronos*) and its deeper, eternal sense (*aion*) is articulated by *kairos*—the time in which eternity emerges and breaks the succession of chronology's instants.

"Earthly men" become divine when "entirely transfigured," so "this earthly life swings up into heaven" (Müntzer, *Testimony* 278). Again, the inner transformation of the Christian and the outer transformation of society converge. From there, an eschatological principle follows: the establishment of an order in which it is possible to live as if our life takes place in heaven. The time of this establishment is "now." The eternal is neither in the future to be realized nor solely within the soul but is present in every "now." The translation of Luke 17:21 leads to two different interpretations: "The kingdom of God is within you [ἐντὸς ὑμῶν]." This interpretation can have an intimist and quietist outcome; instead, when ἐντὸς ὑμῶν is translated as "among you," "in the midst of you," or "near to hand," there may be social or millenarian implications. The former translation, common to many English editions and certainly more appropriate to the modern individualist spirit and a purely private understanding of salvation, was also Luther's translation: "The kingdom of God is within you [*das Reich Gottes ist inwendig in euch*]." The latter, more eschatological interpretation, can be paired with Mark 1:15: "The time [καιρὸς] has come, and the kingdom of God has drawn near." In Müntzer's interpretation, the kingdom of God is not postponed to the future. Rather it is "the kingdom of this world" (*Protestation Concerning* 371) situated in the tension between the "now" and the "not-yet." The kingdom is anticipated in the uprising of the humble. The inner transformation of man and the outer transformation of the world have already begun. It is not a matter of achieving them in the future, but of defending them in the now.

In the *Fürstenpredigt*, Müntzer takes from Daniel (2:34) the image of the cornerstone that has come loose from the mountain. Though initially very small, it will very soon (*gar bald*) fill the whole world. Müntzer overlaps the image of the stone detached from the mountain in Nebuchadnezzar's dream with the image of the cornerstone rejected by the builders. For Müntzer, the church has been fallacious from the beginning, since the stone has always been rejected by those in power. This failure has continued to the present day, that is, to the last reign described by Daniel. The stone that initially fell away "without human hand" (*Interpretation* 232) is the depiction of Jesus Christ. It now coincides with the mystical body of the elect, meaning the discarded of the present time, that is, the poor and the peasants. The stone "is a large one now; the poor laity and the peasants have a much sharper eye for it" than the princes (245).

The reading and interpretation of Nebuchadnezzar's dream serves two additional functions. In the biblical account, the soothsayers called on by Nebuchadnezzar to reconstruct the dream fail and are put to death. The first parallel is with the theological flatterers of the princes. It is Daniel who provides the explanation of the dream. Contrary to the Lutheran Reformation, which left the interpretation of the Bible to theologians and scholars reading a "dumb" text,[3] Müntzer aimed to elevate dreams and visions as a means of continuing revelation within the community. Dreams and visions were democratic forms through which the community could continue the work of revelation. When Müntzer refers to a new Daniel, it is important to understand that he is not referring to an individual, much less himself, but rather to a collective Daniel embodied by the community.

The reforms of Luther and Müntzer diverged. By contrasting God's "living voice" with the "dead words of Scripture," Müntzer departs from the course of the Lutheran Reformation to reconnect with the spirit of German mysticism, to Meister Eckhart and Johann Tauler, for whom God speaks directly to all, and the order of God implanted in all creatures is more important than the Scriptures (Rowland 45–47). The time of revelation is not the past tense, not frozen in Scripture, but in the present tense of the community and of a God who speaks. Faith does not require a church or the exegesis of theologians. Rather it is encapsulated "in the hearts of the elect throughout the earth" (Müntzer, *Collected Works* III). Hence, wrote Müntzer, "even if someone were born a Turk, he still has the beginning of the same faith" (III). The elect are those who open their hearts and minds to God, regardless of their social status and religion. They can also be Muslims or Jews (Drummond 168). The universality of faith and continuous revelation underlie the democratic spirituality on which Müntzer sought to restore a just order of the living. So Müntzer developed the hidden political kernel of mysticism (Goertz 103–10).

It is useful to recall the terms of conflict: Luther's praise of submission to the authority of the princes is contrasted with the peasants' revolt against an unjust order. Similarly, his exhortation to the internalization of the kingdom of God should be understood as contrasting with the apocalyptic time of the "transformation of the world" (Müntzer, *Interpretation* 244). The apocalyptic principle, observed Jacob Taubes, "combines within a form-destroying and a forming power" (10–11). The two principles operate together. If the destructive element (*Gestalt-zerstörend*) is absent, then the positivity of a frozen order prevails. However, if the forming element (*Gestaltend*) anticipated in a new covenant (*neuer Bund*) is missing, then change precipitates into an empty nothingness and a revolution of nihilism (II). Luther and Müntzer are personifications of these tensions, different and incompatible attempts to balance the conflicting forces. Paul had previously faced this issue and attempted to integrate messianic enthusiasm into a communitarian framework that promised some form of unstable stability. Luther was intimidated by instability and chose order and obedience, while Müntzer taught his followers not to fear the instability and the power of the princes. Instability was necessary for the consolidation of the new order anticipated by the elect.

The "time of harvest is certainly here" (Müntzer, *Testimony* 312). This passage, which refers to several scriptural passages (Joel 3:13, Mark 4:29, Revelation 14:14–19, Matthew 9:37, Matthew 13:30), becomes a political exhortation in the April 1525 letter to the League at Allstedt: "The time is now [*Es ist Zeit*]" (Müntzer, *An ehemalige Mitglieder* 413). It is the time (*kairos*) for intervention and change. This time cannot be measured by clocks. Instead, it is characterized by an outer dimension that is measurable by the level of corruption of time, and by an inner dimension that is measurable in human change, in the emptying (*Entwerden*) by the fear of God, and in the collective transformation that gives rise to the emancipated man (*gelassener Mensch*), free from all subjection, restraint, and fear of the people and authorities of this world (Müntzer, *Interpretation* 235). These dimensions intersect in the now of the peasants' revolt. And it would be a crime not to seize the opportunity of this change. *Kairos* is not an apocalyptic event projected into the future: "Now is the favorable time, now is the day of salvation" (II Cor. 6:2). If the time (*kairos*) is now, the servants are truly free. The time (*chronos*), in which the slave is subject to the master, must be ended. Luther neutralizes the tension between the two temporalities by secularizing the "calling" in the notion of *Beruf*. In the dominant Reformation, the messianic intonation of the term *call* (*klesis*), which divides time into opposing overlapping temporalities, eternal and worldly time, is dissolved: the "individual should remain once and for all in the station and calling in which God had placed him" (Weber 44). The servant should remain a servant. The acceptance of the existing situation is reinforced by the dilation and neutralization of the messianic temporality of the calling: "Since everyone was simply waiting for the coming of the Lord, there was nothing to do but remain in the station and in the worldly occupation in which the call of the Lord had found him, and labour as before" (Weber 43). As Max Weber pointed out, the Protestant ethic is married to the ethic of capitalism. It is only necessary to add that this union was celebrated with the blood of the peasants, that is, suppressing the trajectory undertaken by them.

While Müntzer still sought the support of the princes in the *Fürstenpredigt* at Allstedt Castle on July 13, 1524, a few months later it became clear that this support had failed to materialize, and that the community had to take control of its own destiny. The time had come because the community had already taken the sword back into its own hands. Müntzer followed the community, he did not lead it. Resistance is first of all duty, a duty to godly law, but also to a just order to be preserved or restored. The peasants claimed a freedom regulated both by biblical bonds and legal obligations, such as the "Eleven Articles of Mühlhausen" drafted by Müntzer and Heinrich Pfeiffer in 1524 for the Ewiger Bund Gottes. The experiment was short-lived, but it was resumed in April 1525, when Müntzer and Pfeiffer marched with four hundred followers and the rainbow flag to Mühlhausen, where they set up the Eternal Council (Ewiger Rat). Mühlhausen was an experiment in self-government and popular control over governing bodies and resources. The peasants' military troops also exhibited a similar democratic spirit. Commanders were elected and could be dismissed, and provisioning took place only at the expense of the convents and nobility. "In this way," Bensing wrote, "the establishment of the future society dreamed of by Müntzer was anticipated within the ranks of the peasants during the war" (151–53). As part of his political agenda, Müntzer aimed to acquire the territory encompassing a radius of forty-six modern miles around Mühlhausen, which was referred to as "X meyl weges umb Mollhhawsen," including the land situated in Hessen (Müntzer, "Interrogation" 437; Müntzer, *Thomas-Müntzer-Ausgabe* 3: 272). For daring to show the concrete possibility of a different order of things, the peasants' institutions were crushed and their memory erased.

All of Müntzer's theology is characterized by the transfer of power from the Catholic Church, the learned Lutheran theologians, and the princes to the community. In Müntzer's democratic theology, God has not stopped speaking but is the living word, the permanent revelation of the community, which works through dreams and visions. Authority is and must remain in the hands of the community. Western modernity arises in this tension. It is not the tension between Luther and Müntzer. It is not a philological battle over Scripture. It is a clash between distinct trajectories. On the one hand, there are the peasant revolts that culminated in the great battle of Frankenhausen in 1525, driven by their communities, their demands for self-government, for a just and godly order, and common ownership of land. On the other hand, there is the conjunction between the German princes and the Reformation. *Individualism* versus community. *The state* versus local self-government. *Private property* versus communal control of property. Here is the secular trinity of modernity, sanctified by the Protestant spirit. And yet the Peasants' War shows an outcome of feudalism that is not the centralization of sovereignty and individual private property, but the dispersion of sovereignty into political units and forms of ownership democratized by communal control and common relations of use. It shows a practice of democracy in terms of participation and control of those in power. It shows a different anthropological configuration.

In May 1525, in a confession extracted under torture, Müntzer affirmed the principle that *omnia sunt communia* (all things are in common), and that everyone is given according to his needs (*Thomas-Müntzer-Ausgabe* 3: 271). This principle, whether or not it was actually stated by Müntzer, lived a life of its own. In a short text written in late May and early June 1525, Melanchthon summarized Müntzer's "devil doctrine" in the principles of the communion of all goods, the annihilation of all instituted authority, the end of princes and kings, and the false doctrine of the presence of God's signs even in dreams (*Die Histori* 28). Melanchthon's text is also an example of creative historiography. His *Histori* was written a hundred miles away from where Müntzer was tortured and finally killed on May 27. Despite this distance, Melanchthon reports several speeches given by Müntzer before, during, and after the battle of Frankenhausen. However, fabrication does not constitute the most important point. Melanchthon's text, together with *Dreadful History and Judgement of God on Thomas Müntzer*, written by Luther in May 1525, is characterized by two precise qualities. First, Müntzer's defeat is read and interpreted as God's judgment on the devil. Both Luther and Melanchthon refer to Müntzer as the embodiment of evil. The exchange of name-calling was common. Müntzer had previously referred to Luther as "Easy-Living Flesh in Wittenberg," "Doctor Ludicrous," and "Doctor Liar," among other names. In turn, Luther described Müntzer as the devil, the Satan cast out of Zwickau. The difference is not just one of tone. Luther and Melanchthon demonized the enemy using politicized moral and theological categories. This logic would continue for centuries and still characterizes domestic and international politics today. The enemy became the embodiment of evil to be destroyed for the establishment of an order, whose justice was grounded in the opposition to evil. A new political theology was taking shape. Second, as Luther did on numerous occasions, Melanchthon recalls Paul 13 and reiterates the obligation to obey authority because God punishes disobedience and resistance. If Müntzer and the peasants could still appeal to a legal system that left room for the right of resistance, Luther closed that space and inaugurated the political theology of modernity. Melanchthon and Luther, along with the theorists of political and legal modernity, worked to block a tradition in which earthly justice was questionable in the light of custom and divine law; a tradition in which resistance was a political means of restoring and negotiating justice; a tradition in which private property did not constitute an absolute right of the owner. The thinkers of political and legal modernity produced concepts that were polemically oriented against this tradition and its possibilities.

The principle of *omnia sunt communia* was not an invention. It was rooted in a well-known tradition of natural law (*iure naturale omnia sunt communia* or *iure divino omnia esse communia*) (*Summa Parisiensis*, Distinctio VIII). *Das Buch der hundert Kapitel* refers to the Romanistic principle of "this is mine" and "this is yours" as contrary to friendship and natural divine law (*naturlich gotlich Recht*) (Franke 248). The rural commune established rigorous communal regulations concerning property rights. Müntzer is the spokesman for a tradition that goes back in history to the *Acts of the Apostles* and into the future.[4] Luther asserted that *"non est juris naturae communio rerum"* (the community of goods is not in accordance with natural law) in order to neutralize the subversive charge of the natural law tradition that was still vital in peasants' uprisings (*Tagebuch* 165). In opposition, in the *Schutzrede*, Müntzer condemns the lords' appropriation of all creatures, including "the fish in the water, the birds in the air, the plants on the face of the earth" (*Vindication* 335). Referring to Isaiah 5:8, Müntzer argues that by appropriating what is common, which cannot actually be appropriated, princes and lords violate the divine commandment not to steal. Therefore, the poor have a duty to insurrection.

This story of the early modern peasant uprising is not one of a history bound to fail, but of the invocation of concrete possibilities that were violently repressed and neutralized by the new legal and political order that took shape with the emergence of the modern state and the grammar of individual rights. The Peasants' War shows the making of modern political concepts and their polemical nature. In showing their making, it also shows their possible unmaking contained in the concrete possibilities endorsed by the insurgent peasantry. For this reason, it is an origin. Not an end. ∎

Massimiliano Tomba is professor in the History of Consciousness Department at the University of California, Santa Cruz. He is the author of many articles and books. Among them are *Marx's Temporalities* (2012) and *Insurgent Universality: An Alternative Legacy of Modernity* (2019).

NOTES

1 "Let every person be subject to the governing authorities; for there is no authority except from God, and those authorities that exist have been instituted by God" (Romans 13:1).

2 "For the one who loves another [ἕτερον] has fulfilled the law" (Romans 13:8).

3 In 1521 Müntzer signed the *Prague Manifesto* with these words: "Thomas Müntzer wants no dumb God to worship but one who speaks" (*Protestation Concerning* 371).

4 Acts 2:44: "All who believed were together and had all things in common [*omnia communia habeant*]." See also Acts 4:32–34.

WORKS CITED

Baumann, Franz Ludwig, eds. *Akten zur Geschichte des Deutschen Bauernkrieges aus Oberschwaben.* Freiburg im Breisgau: Herder'sche Verlagshandlung, 1877.

Bensing, Manfred. *Thomas Müntzer und der Thüringen Aufstand 1525.* Berlin: Deutscher Verlag der Wissenschaften, 1966.

Blickle, Peter. "Bundschuh." In vol. 2 of *Lexikon des Mittelalters*, 936–37. Munich: Artemis Verlag, 1982.

Blickle, Peter. *Der Bauernkrieg: Die Revolution des Gemeinen Mannes*. Munich: Verlag C. H. Beck, 1998.

Blickle, Peter. *The Revolution of 1525*. Baltimore: Johns Hopkins University Press, 1981.

Bloch, Ernst. *Thomas Müntzer als Theologe der Revolution*. Munich: Kurt Wolff Verlag, 1921.

Bräuer, Siegfried, and Günter Vogler. *Thomas Müntzer: Neu Ordnung machen in der Welt*. Munich: Gütersloher Verlagshaus, 2016.

Brunner, Otto. *Land and Lordship: Structures of Governance in Medieval Austria*. Philadelphia: University of Pennsylvania Press, 1992.

Buszello, Horst. "The Common Man's View of the State in the German Peasant War." In *The German Peasant War of 1525, New Viewpoints*, edited by Bob Scribner and Gerhard Benecke, 109–23. London: Routledge, 1979.

Drummond, Andrew. *The Dreadful History and Judgement of God on Thomas Müntzer: The Life and Times of an Early German Revolutionary*. London: Verso, 2024.

Engels, Friedrich. *The Peasant War in Germany*. New York: International Publishers, 1926.

Franke, Annelore, ed. *Das Buch der hundert Kapitel und der vierzig Statuten des sogenannten Oberrheinischen Revolutionärs*. Berlin: VEB Deutscher Verlag der Wissenschaften, 1967.

Franz, Günther. *Der deutsche Bauernkrieg*. Darmstadt, Germany: Wissenschaftliche Buchgesellschaft, 1977.

Franz, Günther. *Quellen zur Geschichte des Bauernkrieges*. Darmstadt, Germany: Wissenschaftliche Buchgesellschaft, 1963.

Goertz, Hans-Jürgen. *Thomas Müntzer: Apocalyptic Mystic and Revolutionary*. Edinburgh: T&T Clark, 1993.

Günther, Gerhard. "Altes Recht, Göttliches Recht, und Römisches Recht in der Zeit der Reformation und des Bauernkrieges." *Wissenschaftliche Zeitschrift der Karl-Marx-Universität* 14 (1965): 427–34.

Hegel, Georg Wilhelm Friedrich. *The Philosophy of History*. 1837; repr., Kitchner, ON: Batoche, 2001.

Hobbes, Thomas. *Leviathan. Sive de materia, forma, et potestate civitatis ecclesiasticae et civilis* (Latin edition, 1670). Vol. 3 of *Opera philosophica*, edited by W. Molesworth. London: Apud Joannem Bohn, 1841.

Hobbes, Thomas. *Leviathan*. Oxford: Oxford University Press, 1998.

Kern, Fritz. *Kingship and Law in the Middle Ages*. Oxford: Basil Blackwell, 1939.

Laube, Adolf. "Precursors of the Peasant War: *Bundschuh* and *Armer Konrad*." In *The German Peasant War of 1525*, edited by Janos Bak, 49–53. New York: Routledge, 2013.

Linebaugh, Peter. *The Magna Carta Manifesto*. Berkeley: University of California Press, 2008.

Luther, Martin. *Ermahnung zum Frieden auf die zwölf Artikel der Bauernschaft in Schwaben* (*Admonition to Peace Concerning the Twelve Articles of the Peasants*). 1525. In vol. 18 of *Martin Luthers Werke: Kritische Gesamtausgabe*, 279–334. Weimar, Germany: Hermann Böhlaus Nachfolger, 1908.

Luther, Martin. *Tagebuch aus das Jahr 1538*. Edited by Anton Lauterbach. Dresden: Verlag von Justus Naumann's Buchhandlung, 1872.

Luther, Martin. *Von der Freiheit eines Christenmenschen*. 1520. In vol. 7 of *Martin Luthers Werke: Kritische Gesamtausgabe*, 12–38. Weimar, Germany: Hermann Böhlaus Nachfolger, 1908.

Luther, Martin. *Wider den Reubischen und Mördischen Rotten der Bauern* (*Against the Robbing and Murdering Hordes of Peasants*). 1525. In vol. 18 of *Martin Luthers Werke: Kritische Gesamtausgabe*, 344–61. Weimar, Germany: Hermann Böhlaus Nachfolger, 1908.

Mayenburg, David von. *Gemeiner Mann und Gemeines Recht: Die Zwölf Artikel und das Recht des ländlichen Raums im Zeitalter des Bauernkrieges*. Frankfurt: Vittorio Klostermann, 2018.

Melanchthon, Philip. *Die Histori Thome Muntzers, des anfengers der Döringischen Vffurur, sehr nutzlich zulesen* (Hagenau, 1525). In *Die lutheraniscehn Pamphlete gegen Thomas Müntzer*, edited by Ludwig Fischer, 27–42. Tübingen: Max Niemeyer Verlag, 1976.

Melanchthon, Philip. "Gutachten über die 12 Artikel." In Franz, *Quellen*, 179–88.

Müntzer, Thomas. *An ehemalige Mitglieder des Allstedter Bundes* (April 26, 1525). In vol. 2 of Müntzer, *Thomas-Müntzer-Ausgabe*, 403–15.

Müntzer, Thomas. *The Collected Works of Thomas Müntzer*. Translated and edited by Peter Matheson. Edinburgh: T&T Clark, 1988.

Müntzer, Thomas. *Interpretation of the Second Chapter of Daniel* (*Auslegung des zweiten Kapitels des Buches Daniel. Fürstenpredigt*, 1524). In Müntzer, *Collected Works*, 230–52.

Müntzer, Thomas. "Interrogation and 'Recantation' of Müntzer." In Müntzer, *Collected Works*, 433–40.

Müntzer, Thomas. *A Protestation Concerning the Situation in Bohemia* (*Prager Sendbrief: Der Bemen Sache betreffende Protestation*) (1521) In Müntzer, *Collected Works*, 362–71.

Müntzer, Thomas. *The Testimony of Luke and the Exposé of False Faith* (*Gezeugnis des ersten Kapitels des Lukasevangelium*) (1524). In Müntzer, *Collected Works*, 260–323.

Müntzer, Thomas. *Thomas-Müntzer-Ausgabe: Kritische Ausgabe*. 3 vols. Leipzig: Sächsische Akademie der Wissenschaften zu Leipzig, 2017.

Müntzer, Thomas. *Vindication and Refutation of the Unspiritual Soft-Living Flesh in Wittenberg* (*Hochverursachte Schutzrede*, 1524). In Müntzer, *Collected Works*, 327–50.

Ranke, Leopold von. *History of the Reformation in Germany*. London: Routledge, 1905.

Roper, Lyndal. "Emotions and the German Peasants' War of 1524–26." *History Workshop Journal* 92 (2021): 51–81.

Rosenkranz, Albert. *Der Bundschuh: Die Erhebungen des südwestdeutschen Bauernstandes in den Jahren 1493–1517*. Heidelberg: Carl Winters Universitätsbuchhandling, 1927.

Rowland, Christopher. *Radical Prophet: The Mystics, Subversives, and Visionaries Who Strove for Heaven on Earth*. London: I. B. Tauris, 2017.

Sabean, David Warren. *Landbesitz und Gesellschaft am Vorabend des Bauernkrieges*. Stuttgart: Gustav Fisher Verlag, 1972.

Schmidt, Irmgard. *Das göttliche Recht und seine Bedeutung im deutschen Bauernkrieg*. Jena, Germany: Verlag der Frommanischen Buchhandlung, 1939.

Schmitt, Carl. *Political Theology*. Chicago: University of Chicago Press, 2005.

Scott, Tom, and Bob Scribner. *The German Peasants' War: A History in Documents*. New York: Humanity, 1991.

Sea, Thomas F. "The German Princes' Response to the Peasants' Revolt of 1525." *Central European History* 40, no. 2 (2007): 219–40.

Sprandel, Rolf. "Über das Problem neuen Rechts im früheren Mittelalter." *Zeitschrift der Savigny-Stiftung für Rechtsgeschichte* 48 (1962): 117–37.

Sreenivasan, Govind P. "The Social Origins of the Peasants' War of 1525 in Upper Swabia." *Past and Present* 171 (2001): 30–65.

Stein, Peter. *Roman Law in European History*. Cambridge: Cambridge University Press, 1999.

Stern, Alfred. "Das römische Recht und der deutsche Bauernkrieg von 1525." *Zeitschrift für schweizerische Geschichte* 14 (1934): 20–29.

Strauss, Gerald. *Law, Resistance, and the State: The Opposition to Roman Law in Reformation Germany*. Princeton, NJ: Princeton University Press, 1986.

The Summa Parisiensis on the Decretum Gratiani. Edited by Terence P. McLaughlin. Toronto: PIMS, 1952.

Taubes, Jacob. *Occidental Eschatology*. Stanford, CA: Stanford University Press, 2009.

Weber, Max. *The Protestant Ethic and the Spirit of Capitalism*. London: Routledge, 2001.

Whitman, James Q. *The Legacy of Roman Law in the Germanic Romantic Era*. Princeton, NJ: Princeton University Press, 1990.

Anne Norton

"This Is My Body"

Thomas Müntzer, Prophetic People, and Embodied
Sovereignty

ABSTRACT The author argues that Müntzer offers an unrecognized conception of sovereignty as popular, disseminate, and prophetic. The grounding for this conception of sovereignty can be found in Müntzer's use of common, vulgar, and scatological language, and the
ways in which his use departs radically from Luther's.

KEYWORDS sovereignty, body, prophecy, people, common

There should be, in this issue, at this time, no need to defend the memory of
Thomas Müntzer. Nevertheless, out of respect for his memory and hope that
his work continues, I offer this account of why I read Thomas Müntzer. I read
him because he shepherded one of the most democratic of rebellions. I read
him to see where his faith in democracy came from. I read him to learn how
he fashioned religion into a sword. I read to hear what he said to the princes
he opposed and what he said to the common people he fought for. I have read
him many times now, though I still have access to only a small part of what
he wrote. I want him to be read more widely. Read him so that you can see the
costs for dissent in his time. Read him for the prophetic democratic. Read
him for his courage.

Müntzer's earthy, coarse, common invective opens to a rare and unrecognized understanding of popular sovereignty. This is not the sovereignty of
The People but the sovereignty of people: embodied, suffering, prophetic,
divine. Müntzer's faith that ordinary people can prophecy testifies to the
power of democratic demands. Müntzer's conviction that people—Christian
or not—carry the divine within them testifies to the possibility of a form of
sovereignty that is carried by the people not only in their unity but in their
separate, singular bodies.

HISTORY of the PRESENT ▪ A Journal of Critical History ▪ 15:1 ▪ April 2025
DOI: 10.1215/21599785-11561498 © 2025 Duke University Press

Begin, then, with the presence of the body in the words of Müntzer, who spoke with and of and for the people, and Luther, the man who set himself against them. One who reads the speeches and correspondence, remonstrances and sermons, of the Reformation in Germany cannot fail to be struck by the presence of the body: the smelly, rotten, pissing, farting, defecating body. The modern ear and eye expect the ethereal from the religious, especially the erudite religious. Not so the theological disputants of Wittenberg, Prague, and Allstedt. They are earthly, they are coarse, they are vulgar. Their invective startles the more modest ears of modern scholars.

These are not ranting releases of emotion, nor are they a kind of intellectual slumming, meant to reach the common man. Erik Erikson took special note of Luther's profane and scatological invective, an interest that he shares with all of Luther's biographers. Luther, he writes, could be so vulgar that he became easy game for the priest and the psychiatrist, both of whom quote him with relish: "Thou shalt not write a book unless you have listened to the fart of an old sow, to which you should open your mouth wide and say 'Thanks to you, pretty nightingale; do I hear a test which is for me?'" (Erikson 33). The fat farting sow appears so often in Luther that Erikson concludes that "there was a soft spot for the sow so large" that it should be considered "one of Luther's identity elements." In later years, "His colorful earthiness sometimes turned into plain porcography" (Erikson 33). Luther, in short, saw himself lying in the gutter and the manure, like the unredeemed sow. The image is a rich one. Who among us has not wallowed unthinkingly in earthy pleasures? Who has not grunted and eaten and farted and defecated? What does it mean, then, to open one's ears and mouth to all the simplicity, all the unredeemed, unmediated, materiality of the wallowing sow? Perhaps it means that before you write a book you should listen to the body. That is what we shall do here.

Whether in human or in swinish form, Luther was (even by medieval standards) preoccupied with defecation. He claimed, at a dinner, to have been visited by the Holy Spirit on the toilet. At another dinner (what a table companion he must have been) he announced, "I am like a ripe shit . . . and the world is a gaping asshole. We will let go of each other soon enough" (206). It is too simple, and if one listens to the sow, misleading, to read this as simple disdain for a dirty, contemptible world. One takes one's corporeality with one, even after death. One comes from the earth and to earth one returns: ashes to ashes, dust to dust. The eaters are eaten, we become food for worms.

The rectum was gateway, battleground, and weapon for Luther. One confronted the devil by farting in his mouth or telling him, "I have shit in the pants and you can hang them around your neck and wipe your mouth with it" (244–45). This image has had a late revival during the New York trial of Donald Trump, most notably when Trump's former lawyer Michael Cohen referred to him as Von ShitzInPantz. The Pope, the devil's servant, was "*Furzesel*," fart ass, and he had the Holy Mother Church "as a whore, giving rectal birth to a race of devils" (246). Approaching his death, Luther would see the devil sitting on a drainpipe, exposing his ass (59).

Anyone who has gazed at the paintings of Hieronymus Bosch will recognize the earthy vulgarity of Luther's invective, cast in another form. If Luther was particularly drawn to the scatological, he nevertheless remained within the boundaries of custom and convention. As Philippe Ariès teaches us, the people of Luther's time were far more intimate, perhaps more comfortable, and certainly more engaged, with the body in its living, dying, and decaying splendor.

Scatological invective was only one of the rhetorical codes and styles Luther mastered. He is also the writer (arguably the inventor) of a German vernacular that ranged from the childlike charm of hymn and folk song to the elegance of Biblical translations. Nietzsche, Grimm, and many more have seen a miraculous purity and beauty in the German of Luther's vernacular Bible. Those qualities, made manifest in its extensive circulation, gave it a profound influence on modern German. Erikson observed that "Beside his diatribes of hate and blasphemous filth, [Luther] wrote lyrics which have the power and the simplicity of folksong" (233). Luther's rhetorical and authorial range makes his choice of the scatological deliberate and telling.

Luther's rhetorical coprophilia is largely peripheral to Erikson's analysis, but he notes that it was at once conventional and peculiarly indicative of the tensions in Luther's psyche. There are other tensions evident here. One is central to Christianity. Christianity, both popular and doctrinal, insists on the primacy of the soul and the spiritual. Christians seeking the divine have sought it through the mortification of the flesh in penitential and ascetic practices. Embodiment is that which is to be overcome, and that which enables the overcoming. The Incarnation makes God an embodied being: born from a woman, suckled at her breast, eating and defecating, perhaps having sex (though that remains a silence), and, above all, suffering and dying. The belief in an incarnate deity opens the possibility that it is in and as embodied beings that one becomes one with the divine. That meeting is enacted and reenacted in the sacrament of the Eucharist. The communicant consumes the host, "the Body of Christ." As Spinoza irreverently but accurately asked his convert pupil, "O youth deprived of understanding, who has bewitched you into believing that the Supreme and Eternal is eaten by you and held in your intestines?" (Spinoza 416). Consuming the Eucharist brings the divine body within the bounds of the human, within the individual body, and as it does so, it brings the individual body within the body of the church. The knot of transubstantiation binds together individual and collective, human and divine, the sacred and profane, the material and the spiritual. Luther's doctrine of consubstantiation sits uneasily between Catholic transubstantiation and more radical Protestant conceptions of the bread and wine as wholly symbolic. How much of the earthly, how much of the body, was present in the divine was a tension that animated Protestant sectarianism and troubled Luther. The question of how much was divine, how much human, in Jesus; how the human and divine were (or were not) joined in him, gave rise to one heresy (and one orthodoxy) after another, long before the appearance of Protestant sectarians.

Other tensions accompany both these religious controversies and other, more earthly political struggles. Those are the tensions that accompany the question of equality. There is no one so rich, so powerful, so beautiful, so wise, that they do not shit. In that, as in breathing, all are equal. Many observers, educated and uneducated, refined and vulgar, have seen this common human need as a marker of equality. Michelet wrote of Louis Quatorze, afflicted with an anal fistula, "Nature permitted herself to take him in the place where all men are humiliated. . . . This brazen nature was telling him 'You are a man. You are human.'" The word links humus to earth and dissolution, "ashes to ashes, dust to dust," and recalls that common mortality in which, as Hobbes observed, we are all equal (Barthes 136–37).

Luther was, initially, a critic, if not an opponent of princes, marking their secular rule as antithetical to Christianity. "Some time ago I wrote a pamphlet to the German nobility. In it I set out their tasks and duties as Christians. How much notice they took of it is plain for all to see." In a closing broadside that anticipates Müntzer he wrote, "Long may they remain princes and never become Christians." He would not hold to that view. He would take the side of the princes against the people. He would come down decisively against equality. By 1525 Luther was inveighing "Against the Robbing, Murdering Hordes of Peasants." He wrote, "Therefore let everyone who can, smite, slay, and stab, secretly or openly, remembering that nothing can be more poisonous, hurtful, or devilish than a rebel. . . . For baptism does not make men free in body and property, but in soul; and the gospel does not make goods common . . . there is not a devil left in hell; they have all gone into the peasants" (Luther, "Against" 3).

Luther's scatological invective aimed at powerful enemies, but it did not seek equality. Müntzer did likewise and otherwise. Like Luther, Müntzer was a master of invective, and as Alberto Toscano memorably wrote, with

Müntzer "scatology and eschatology are never too far apart" (in Müntzer xi). These are not merely rhetorical extremes. In a moment when a sacred text was newly cast into the vernacular, a marked turn to the vernacular signaled a change not simply of code and valence but of loyalties and commitments. This was the speech of the common man. For Müntzer it was more, it was the speech of the commons. Müntzer kept his Latin to the end, holding steadfast under torture to declare *omnia sunt communia*. When he turned to the vernacular, the profane, the coarse, and the vulgar, it was as an affirmation of equality, to raise the poor and bring down the mighty. If the German vernacular word for the common, *gemein*, held connotations (as it still does) of "nasty," "vulgar," "beastly," and "coarse," those attributes would be if not erased, elevated in *gemeinschaft* and *gemeinsamkeit*.

The greed and excesses of the wealthy and privileged were written on their bodies for Müntzer. One of his most common terms of derision is "chubby cheeks" (Müntzer 59). In German as in English, that can signify the face or the ass. In either case, the baby face or fat ass is simultaneously demeaned and charged: demeaned as infantile, charged with greed and excess. Müntzer's opponents in the clergy have "snouts," they are "condemned with skin and hair to eternal damnation" (3, 5). Luther, the indulged client of princes, becomes "Brother Fattened-Swine" and "Brother Soft-Life" (*Sanftleben*) (26, 46).

Inequalities of wealth were perhaps the most common of Müntzer's targets, but they were not exclusive. His vulgar invective was directed at the arrogance of intellect as well as that of wealth, at the "donkey cunt doctor of theology," the "scrotum-like," "diarrhea-maker" priests, and the "Nero-like" "wooden pope and chamber pot at the brothel of Rome." Luther was "Father Pussy-foot (*Leisetritt*)" and "Doctor Liar." The priests, Müntzer warned his people, "will shit on you with a new logic, twisting the word of God" (78–79, 2, 7, 8, 9, x). God himself, Müntzer declares in an intensified paraphrase of Jeremiah 23, had disdain for these because "they usurp my words and make them putrid in their stinking lips and whorish throats" (2). They stink, all of them, the powerful and their military minions, for these "enemies of the cross have crapped their courage into their pants" (35).

This failure is moral and political, for these cannot be separated. "Parsons are lords," Müntzer writes, who only "devour, swill, and steal, day and night" in order to "get many fiefs." They are "profit-seeking and interest-boosting" (6). They "gladly take golden guilders with great devotion." In a phrase still resonant, "they do not need a hundredth part of what they take" (61).

References to the 99 percent have a long and honorable history. So, too, does the rainbow flag. Contemporary queer users of the banner rarely know its origins. It is known that the rebellious forces Müntzer marched with used a rainbow flag (though no examples survive) and that Müntzer had a role in its design. That is hardly surprising, as the rainbow marked the covenant in the scriptural story of Noah. The long gap between 1525 and 1978 when the rainbow flag emerges as the "gay flag" may have been mediated by the flag of the International Cooperative Alliance of the 1920s. This was apt, as it recalled the commitment of the 1525 uprisings to common ownership. Both Greece and Italy are said to have used rainbow flags as signs of peace, a practice that was adopted in the student uprisings of the sixties. For Müntzer and the revolutionaries, the flag recalled God writing a covenant with man on the sky. For those who have followed, knowingly or unknowingly, in Müntzer's footsteps and under his banner, it has come to mark commitments to equality and emancipation.

Müntzer's God was a god of writing as well as prophetic speech. God left his mark on Cain, on the sky in the rainbow after the great flood, and on Abraham and the children of Abraham. So too did the devil or the demons of their own evildoing leave their marks on the bodies of the corrupt. Divine or demonic, the text could be read on the body. The greedy got chubby cheeks, soft hands, and bodies unused to labor. The decadent decayed. Their greed, their arrogance, their lying, all leave their marks on the people. The faithful are made coarse by the teachings of the corrupt. They thirst for knowledge, God speaks to them, but they cannot be certain of what they hear.

That God inscribed his will on the elect was an old and well-established view of prophecy. When Moses hesitates, unsure of his ability, God tells him, "I will be with thy mouth" (Exodus 4:12).[1] Ezekiel is commanded, "Son of man, eat that which thou findest, eat this roll. . . . So I opened my mouth and he caused me to eat that roll. And he said unto me, cause thy belly to eat, and fill thy bowels with this roll that I give thee" (Ezekiel 3:1–3). Revelations 10:10 states, "And I took the little book out of the angel's hand and ate it up, and it was in my mouth sweet as honey, and as soon as I had eaten it my belly was bitter." These prefigure the sacrament of the Eucharist, to be sure, but they also point to the ability of the divine to take up a dwelling in human bodies, to speak from within the bodies of mankind. They also suggest that prophecy is borne as a burden on and in the bodies of the prophets, for it is bitter in the belly.

It was bitter for Müntzer. The revolutionaries of 1525, like many before and after, put their bodies on the line. They would be killed, wounded, and maimed. They would suffer, as they had suffered before, and that suffering would bear witness. Müntzer would suffer with them.

Müntzer's torture figures prominently (more prominently in the trailer than the film itself) in a 1956 film by Martin Hellberg made in East Germany.

Müntzer's work, and that of his common allies, can find a place in both Christian and Marxist lineages. In both, materiality drives the narrative. The incarnation and crucifixion drive the former. In the Marxist account offered by Hellberg, suffering is inscribed on the bodies of the people, and it is through their bodies that they learn solidarity and drive toward rebellion. It is through their bodies that they act and speak. They resist, they take up arms. They speak with their mouths, to be sure, but in a visual echo of Müntzer's scatological insults, a rebellious peasant confronts a wealthy council member saying, "I bow in salutation, sir council member," then bends over and drops his pants in a universal expression of disdain.

The body was the site of man's equality with man and offered earthly means for expressing that principle. For Müntzer, the body was also the place where God and man met and became one, the site of man's divinity. In part, this reflected an established Christian understanding of Jesus as both the Son of God and the Son of Man. In part, it followed the sacrament of the Eucharist, in doctrine and in ordinary practice. Yet it also reflected Müntzer's beliefs and teaching on human suffering.

The revelation to Moses is prompted by the sight of the suffering people. God says to Moses, "I have surely seen the affliction of my people" and "I have heard their cry" (Exodus 3:7). The New Testament centers on the sacrifice of the Son of God who is also the Son of Man. Perhaps prophecy does not simply come through the mouths of the prophets. Perhaps it comes in and through and as the embodied. Perhaps suffering for others blurs the line between the human and the divine.

"God speaks only in the suffering of creatures," Müntzer writes, "a suffering that the hearts of the unbelievers do not have, because they become more and more hardened." The princes, the wealthy, the scholars and monks and parsons who do not suffer themselves and who are deaf to the suffering of others cannot become "conformed to Christ through suffering" (Müntzer 5). In their suffering bodies the wretched become like the incarnate deity. Their suffering opens them to the divine.

The idea that the sacrament of the Eucharist absorbed the communicant into the body of Christ was often understood as creating the church, the community of the believers, as one body, but it also entailed the idea that divinity lived in the bodies of the people, that they carried it into the world. Like the disciples at Pentecost, they were filled with the Holy Spirit and carried it into the world. This was not, for Müntzer, a rare and distant moment, belonging to a lost age of prophecy. In his *Sermon to the Princes*, he reproaches the hardened privileged and the timid, self-deprecating people: "How shy the people have become! who believe that 'God does not speak any more.'"

He speaks, Müntzer insists, to the suffering. "God despises the powerful and the mighty . . . and he accepts for his service the small" (56–57).

Perhaps prophecy is the place where the divine word and human flesh meet. Perhaps the demands of the body are divine commandments, *mitzvaot*. Perhaps it is in the prophesies of the poor that the divine manifests over and over and over again. Perhaps the divine lives in the people. That thread runs, usually well suppressed, through Christianity. It ran like fire through Müntzer. He closed the Prague Protest with a profession of faith: "Thomas Müntzer will not pray to a dumb God, but rather to one who speaks" (11). God speaks, Müntzer argued, in the voices of living people.

There is "no more certain testimony," Müntzer declared, "than the living speech of God" in the voices of the people. This is one element of politics that Müntzer brought to his people: the conviction that ordinary people carry the divine within themselves. He told them, "That is God's way of working and down to the present day he does not act otherwise" (57).

Müntzer repeatedly insists that living people have divine revelations. He castigates those clergy who "deny that a person can have revelations" and who "speak with the mere words of Scripture" (9). The people of God "should all have revelations" and be "revived by the living voice of God." That is not simply a voice in the ear for Müntzer. "The word of God penetrates the heart, brain, skin, hair, bones, limbs, marrow, juice, force, and power" (7). They will become like gods. Indeed, "they become divine [*vergottet*]" not in a time to come, not in a metaphoric sense, but in "the heart, brain, skin, hair, bones, limbs, marrow, juice, force, and power." Man "fell from being a god to being a creature." They were to recover themselves: "We must hold to it that we carnal, earthly men shall become gods through the incarnation of Christ as man. And so we will be pupils of God with him, being taught and deified by God himself. Yes, indeed, even more, we should be completely and totally transformed into him, so that earthly life revolves into the heavenly" (45).

Eric W. Gritsch, a distinguished Lutheran theologian, nevertheless recognized that the deification of the human was "a description used by the ancient Greek Church fathers" (79). Gritsch insists on regarding Müntzer as a quasi-military leader of the vanguard of the elect, though Müntzer himself insists on a fundamental human equality and does not appear to have ever sought or accepted any title but pastor, and that by the choice of a given group of people. Nor does he appear to have sought or accepted any distinction that might set him apart in his form of life.

Müntzer's understanding of the presence of the divine in the neighbor is an indication that sovereignty need not be unified or uniform. An ambiguously secularized Christianity offers this, consonant with the Pentecostalist model of sovereignty. Islam offers the *umma*, a form of authoritative sovereignty for a democratic people. As Müntzer said, "Do you not think that non-Christians too have a brain in their heads?" (9). One need not look far among the people to find such models: Turks, Jews, and heathens, all people, might return to this divine state. Müntzer insists that even "if one has neither heard nor seen the Bible his whole life long, he could still possess an undeceived Christian faith through the correct teaching of the spirit, as all those had who wrote the holy Scripture without any books" (43). Indeed, "there are many who will be chosen from the wild, strange, heathen." There are "Jewish comrades" as in the past (65). Müntzer's inclusion of Jews as comrades is especially noteworthy when compared with Luther's notoriously virulent anti-Semitism.

Luther's vitriolic pamphlet, "On the Jews and Their Lies," replaced earlier writings in which he had looked toward the conversion of the Jews by a reformed Church and an accessible vernacular Scripture. When that failed, Luther became unremittingly hostile. "On the Jews and Their Lies" is an extraordinary compendium of diverse antisemitic libels in which Luther employs his most scatological and, as Erikson termed it, "porcographic" language. Apologists for Luther note that commentaries on Luther's antisemitism have observed that his Wittenberg church contained the "*Judensau*," a sculptural relief in which Jewish children are suckled at the sow's teats. There is also a man, sometimes identified as a rabbi, who lifts the tail of the pig and leans toward it. The figure leaning toward the sow's tail seems to do exactly as Luther advised and listens to the fart of an old sow. Erikson believed that this sow was "an identity element" for Luther. In this, and in his sharp turn from conversion to annihilation of the Jews, Luther appears to be animated by a complex ambivalence. Who is the sow? Who is the sniffer? Certainly this sculpture was familiar to Luther and to generations of Germans after him. In June 2022 Germany's highest appeals court rejected a Jewish plaintiff's demand that the sculpture be removed under German laws against antisemitism. The court refused, stating that "no law had been violated" (Reuters). In "On the Jews and Their Lies," Luther retails blood libels and stories of Jewish greed and avarice: "Moreover, they are nothing but thieves and robbers who daily eat no morsel and wear no thread of clothing which they have not stolen and pilfered from us by means of their accursed usury. Thus, they live from day to day, together with wife and child, by theft and robbery, as arch thieves and robbers, in the most impenitent security." As a German document it is haunting. Luther wrote, "Eject them forever from this country. For, as we have heard, God's anger with them is so intense that gentle mercy will only tend to make them worse and worse, while sharp mercy will reform them but little. Therefore, in any case, away with them!"

Luther's anger at the Jews mirrored his anger at the peasants. Jews were "nothing but thieves and robbers." So too were the rebellious or revolutionary whom Luther castigated in his pamphlet "Against the Robbing and Murdering Horde of Peasants." Both groups were guilty of crimes against property: Jews in the practice of usury, the revolutionaries in the belief that "*omnia sunt communia.*" Both also presented challenges to Luther's scriptural authority. The Jews were, as Muslims called them, "people of the book," named in the sacred scriptures of Christians as the chosen people of God, possessed of a deep knowledge of those scriptures. Müntzer, also possessed of no small scriptural knowledge, argued that scripture alone was inadequate, but he saw in the Christian scriptures "Jewish comrades."

Those who insist on knowledge of scripture and close their minds to visions among the people will remain ignorant "even if he swallowed a hundred thousand Bibles" (Gritsche 67). Reason and an openness to the spirit are sufficient to open oneself to the divine. For Müntzer, *heilege geist* never lost the connotation of ordinary people possessing minds open to the divine, that anyone, any living human, might become a god.

The tortured body of Christ is an image of suffering as redemptive. This will echo through one popular movement after another, across the Christian world. Martin Luther King's statement is perhaps the simplest: "Unearned suffering is redemptive"[2] Though the Christian prayer, in its reformed Protestant form, asks "our Father" to "forgive us our debts," Christian theology implies that the debt could not simply be forgiven by our creditor father but had to be paid in the flesh. The incarnation and crucifixion provide the currency for redemption. For Müntzer, that suffering provided for more than the payment of debts or the redemption of sins. It made people free. He writes Count Ernst von Mansfeld, "Just tell us, you miserable sack of worms, who made you prince over the people whom God redeemed with his dear blood?" (x). The peasants, the miners, the small merchants, were all free. That freedom, bought by the blood of God, had been stolen by the princes, by lords, clerics, and the wealthy, who sought to bind what God had loosed.

In "On the Jewish Question," Marx called the Revolution of 1525 "the most radical fact of German history" (Müntzer x). Engels called it "the grandest revolutionary effort of the German people" (Blickle 3). Karl Kautsky followed "the red thread" of Müntzer's organizational activity. For the Marxists, Müntzer came before his time. This is the message of the closing frames of Hellberg's 1956 film, which ends with Müntzer's writings being carried into Switzerland and marching rebels singing about unripe fruit and victories in a time yet to come. Kautsky is certainly correct—and reparative—in drawing attention to the geographic breadth of rebellious organization and the infrastructure it established. That activity stretched from the German cities to Prague, Strasbourg, and the Tyrol. Though the uprisings were repressed, they nevertheless established that rebellion not only could occur but had occurred. They gave both an intellectual heritage and the remnants of an organizational infrastructure to subsequent movements. Outside the commitment to historical determinism, Wilhelm Zimmermann, a radical democrat and the first modern historian of the revolution, called it "a battle of freedom against inhuman oppression, of light against darkness" (Blickle 3). In this respect, the revolution lives as a principle of justice and legitimate governance. There is still—as the Zapatistas, *le tute bianche*, and the architects of Red Müntzer days, the novelists and playwrights, testify—a submerged but reachable foundation of memory and aspiration.

The form of government sought by Müntzer and the rebels is often called a theocracy. That is misleading. The rebels sought to follow God, but no more than later revolutionaries would follow natural law. The governance of God was to be found in three sources: in the revealed scripture of the Bible, in the visions sent by God to the living people, and in reason. In Müntzer's work, the last two can modify the first. They are to be ruled "by no dumb god" but by the living speech of the divine in the minds and hearts of the people.

This is no theocracy. This is a vision of the holy spirit descending on all people, living within them. This is a vision of the incarnation where the Son—perhaps the sons—of God opens the way to every son and daughter of man. Such a vision is not difficult to find in the Christian scriptures. It is Jesus who teaches his disciples not to pray to his but to our Father. Pentecost sees divinity spreading like fire. The sacrament of the Eucharist sees divinity as nourishing all the embodied. Müntzer's vision of divinity as present in the heart, brain, skin, hair, bones, limbs, and marrow of ordinary people is a vision of divinity as popular sovereignty and as a commons.

Where all people have access to the divine, all carry sovereignty within them. There are no qualifications of birth, wealth, or education. Each one, however close to the earth, has access to the divine. This is no theocracy. This belongs to the radically democratic and the anarchic.

The practical consequences of this vision of the sovereignty of people are evident in the ways they chose to rule—and to free—themselves. They conduct elections, seek consensus where they can, and appoint all those given authority over them, and they reserve to themselves the imperative mandate. Perhaps the clearest guide to this is the Twelve Articles.

The articles hold that no prince, no lord, no priest, can hold office without the consent of the people. The first article asks that the whole community "choose and appoint its own pastor" and have "authority to depose a pastor who behaves improperly." That daring request, made in all humility ("we humbly ask and beg"), inaugurates the principle of "community consent" that runs through all the articles. The second article declares that the obligation to tithe prescribed in the Old Testament is fulfilled in the New and that nothing therefore can be demanded of the people. Nevertheless, "we wish to pay a just tithe in corn, but only where it is warranted." The article thus endorses forms of taxation and the legitimate ends for common resources. The community would decide the amount and uses of the tithe and abandon a tithe they found unjust. The uses of the tithe would be limited to the maintenance of the (elected) pastor and care for the poor. Together the second and third articles offer a political jubilee, arguing that all are free of debt. The third article makes clear what is being set aside: "It has been the custom until now for lords to treat us as their own property. This is something to be deplored, since Christ redeemed us all by shedding his precious blood, regardless of whether it is a lowly shepherd or the highest in the land, with no exceptions. So the scripture proves that we are, and wish to be, free." They will therefore obey only "our elected and rightful ruler." The sixth, seventh, and eighth articles declare that the terms of labor, leases, rents, and ownership would be decided by contract and the community. Not all property can be owned. The fourth, fifth, and tenth articles establish a large field for the commons. Streams, meadows, farms, and woodlands would be held in common, except where the community decided otherwise. Sales had to be "with the consent of the whole community." The people would decide who could preach, who could act as lord, what could be sold and to whom, what tithes could be collected and how they would be distributed. They charged themselves with providing for their pastors, for the poor. They would protect the community. They would determine the justice of all sentences, punishments, and taxes. Above all, "in the future, we will not allow the lords to oppress us any more" (seventh article). They had this authority from God, not in some distant testament, but in the present. They will "love God" and charged themselves to "see him as our Lord in our neighbor" (third article). The conception of a disseminate divinity might seem abstruse or sophisticated, but it was articulated clearly and seized authoritatively by the rebellious peasants of 1525.

The revolution of 1525 is often referred to as a peasant rebellion, but that is not quite true. It was not a rebellion of peasants alone. It encompassed peasants, smallholders, miners, small merchants, and educated clerics, men and women alike. The miners are a particularly interesting category for several reasons. Their work required courage, perseverance, mutual dependence, and a tolerance of danger. They had preserved elements of Roman organization and customary law. They knew hidden places. They were thus at some advantage in rebellions. The miners of Mansfeld were critical in the rebellion against their lord. Ernst von Mansfeld would ultimately have Müntzer captured, tortured, and killed. It was as a Mansfeld miner that Hans Luther, Martin Luther's father, accumulated the capital to finance his son's education. Martin Luther's rejection of the aims of that education (his father wished him to become a lawyer and official) and his enduring hostility toward his father has its roots in Mansfeld, and it is in response to events in Mansfeld that Luther's hostility to Müntzer erupts.

Neither Müntzer nor the authors of the Twelve Articles thought that they had achieved a perfect common life, but they were on their way to something and covered considerable distance between the space of their oppression and the common life they worked for. Documents like these—declarations, manifestos, constitutions—spread from Strasbourg to the Tyrol, and from Frankenhausen to Augsburg. This is the revolutionary infrastructure Kautsky saw. This political legacy has been disguised, denied, and denigrated, but it has provided foundations to build on. Those of us who are less committed to ideas of progress or a teleological view of history might argue instead that the peasants, miners, and smallholders who rebelled were not building on an infrastructure as much as pulling down the burdensome, repressive, and unjust structures in which lords and clerics had confined them. That is certainly how they portrayed their work, and in that sense they anticipate Thomas Paine's radicalism: "Lay then the axe to the root, and teach governments humanity."

The revolutionaries of 1525, and Müntzer with them, refused the idea that the singular person of a ruling prince could hold sovereignty by the grace of God, still less that such a debased and deceptive person could lay claim to sovereignty as an *imitatio Christi*. The absolutism inherent in the idea of a single sovereign in the person of king or prince has, however, long outlived their refusal. It persists in Carl Schmitt's decisionism. Schmitt himself recognized another form of sovereignty, still modeled on the forms of the Christian trinity. He acknowledged "the reasonable and pragmatic belief that the voice of the people is the voice of God" and that "in democratic thought the people hover above the entire life of the state, just as God does above the world, as the cause and end of all things, as the point from which everything emanates and to which everything returns" (Schmitt 49). This form of sovereignty is omnipresent, but only questionably accessible.

Sheldon Wolin also saw the presence of the sovereign people as episodic. The People are present and active only at moments of crisis and possibility, called into being by need and desire. Democracy is, as Wolin famously argued, fugitive. Are the People present? At those moments, the idea of the People is called forth, but it is not clear whether they are present in a material form, or what becomes of their authority when the fugitive democratic moment ends. It would seem that they, like the Second Coming and the Hidden Imam, lie in stasis, waiting, always confined, though they may appear when the living people call.

The form of sovereignty envisioned by Müntzer and implicit in the Twelve Articles gestures toward a sovereignty that is neither occluded nor episodic. Instead, we can see the lineaments of a popular sovereignty present in the bodies of the living people. This conception of sovereignty differs radically from the conception of "the people" as a unified and uniform whole. It bears a family resemblance to what I have called the pentecostal model of sovereignty (Norton, "Pentecost"). Fugitive democratic moments are possible in embodied popular sovereignty, but sovereignty does not cease to act in their absence. It acts in a dispersed, disseminate form, seeding the democratic. It is embedded in people as they work to rule themselves. Sovereignty is in them, in their bodies. It is in their earthly, material presence, that the right to rule is present in the world.

Think of the people not as an ethereal being hovering above the world, but as present in—present as—the bodies of the living people. No single person holds the whole of sovereignty within, but all the people have access to it and bear it within them (Norton, *Wild Democracy*). They hold it not in pieces, but as channels to an indivisible ocean. Like a Talmudic and Pentecostal fire, this divine excess is not diminished by being shared.

This sovereignty of people speaks a language of prophecy:

> I shall pour out My spirit upon all flesh;
> And your sons and daughters shall prophesy,
> Your old men shall dream dreams,
> Your young men shall see visions;
> And also upon the servants and upon the handmaids
> In those days will I pour out My spirit. (Joel 3:1–2)

Their visions, their dreams, their plans, build democratic worlds. As Massimiliano Tomba has written, these dreams and visions find practical expression in the experiments initiated by revolutionaries: in 1525, in the Paris Commune, in anti-colonial revolutions. Their work is often unfinished, inadequate, undermined, and attacked, but it continues. When it succeeds, it seeds the world. In the glory of their success, they are still people of dreams and vision who look to the *not yet* that they are now free to pursue, that they have yet to achieve. Yet this is sovereignty embodied, and they are the living people. Their sovereignty belongs not only to the not yet of dreams and visions but to the needs of the ordinary human bodies. They speak the language of democratic demands. The needs of ordinary people—for food, for shelter, for care when they are sick, for education, for the tools to build—are not simply needs: they are democratic demands. The revolutionaries of 1525 called for rivers free to fish in, for open forests and meadows. The demands of the living people are no different. They aim simply for the things they need for "life, liberty, and the pursuit of happiness." The demand for bread has been as powerful in driving revolutions as any vision. There is no revolutionary vision, no dream of justice, that does not have the demands of the body at its heart.

From that time to this, many struggles remain. Perhaps Müntzer is still right. Perhaps prophecy has a living voice. The Enlightenment and romantic nationalism after it have taught us to listen for the voice of the people. Perhaps that voice is to be heard not as one unified voice but as many. Perhaps we should listen for the voice of prophecy as Müntzer did, in one person at a time. Perhaps prophecy will be heard not as the Voice of the People but in people's voices. Perhaps these are not the requests of petitioners but the commands of the sovereign. Perhaps we need to sharpen our ears. ∎

Anne Norton is the author of *Wild Democracy: Anarchy, Courage, and Ruling the Law* (2023); *On the Muslim Question* (2013); *95 Theses on Politics, Culture, and Method* (2004); *Leo Strauss and the Politics of American Empire* (2004); *Bloodrites of the Poststructuralists* (2002); and other works on empires and resistance. She is Stacey and Henry Jackson President's Distinguished Professor of Political Science at the University of Pennsylvania. She was educated at the University of Chicago.

ACKNOWLEDGMENTS

I thank Loren Goldman and Massimiliano Tomba for many conversations about Müntzer. I am also grateful to Jack Starobin, who showed me the rich linguistic links between the earth, the human, and humility. That is fertile ground.

NOTES

1   Quotes from the Tanakh are taken from *The Holy Scriptures According to the Masoretic Text* (Philadelphia: Jewish Publication Society), 1955. Quotes from the New Testament are from the King James version.
2   Martin Luther King Jr., "Suffering and Faith," April 27, 1960, King Papers, Stanford University, Stanford, CA, https://kinginstitute.stanford.edu/king-papers/documents /suffering-and-faith (accessed October 6, 2024).

WORKS CITED

Ariès, Philippe. *The Hour of Our Death: The Classic History of Western Attitudes toward Death over the Last One Thousand Years*. Translated by Helen Weaver. New York: Random House, 1982.

Barthes, Roland. *Michelet*. Translated by Richard Howard. New York: Farrar, Strauss and Giroux, 1987.

Blickle, Peter. *The Revolution of 1525: The German Peasants' War from a New Perspective*. Translated by Thomas A. Brady Jr. and H. C. Erik Midelfort. Baltimore: Johns Hopkins University Press, 1977.

Erikson, Erik H. *Young Man Luther: A Study in Psychoanalysis and History*. New York: W. W. Norton, 1958.

Gritsch, Eric W. *Thomas Müntzer: A Tragedy of Errors*. Minneapolis, MN: Fortress, 1989.

Luther, Martin. "Against the Robbing and Murdering Hordes of Peasants." n.d. http://courses.washington.edu/hsteu402/Luther%20against%20Robbing%20Murdering%20Peasants.pdf (accessed August 4, 2024).

Luther, Martin. *On the Jews and Their Lies*. Translator unknown. 1543; excerpted at https://www.jewishvirtuallibrary.org/martin-luther-the-jews-and-their-lies-quotes.

Müntzer, Thomas. *Wu Ming Presents Thomas Müntzer: Sermon to the Princes*. Translated by Michael G. Baylor. London: Verso, 2010.

Norton, Anne. "Pentecost: Democratic Sovereignty in Carl Schmitt." *Constellations* 18, no. 3 (2011): 389–402.

Norton, Anne. *Wild Democracy: Anarchy, Courage, and Ruling the Law*. New York: Oxford University Press, 2023.

Paine, Thomas. *The Rights of Man*. Project Gutenberg, 2003. https://www.gutenberg.org/cache/epub/3742/pg3742-images.html#link2H_4_0003 (accessed October 6, 2024).

Reuters. "Anti-Jewish Medieval Sculpture Can Stay on Church, Top German Court Rules." June 14, 2022. https://www.reuters.com/world/europe/anti-jewish-medieval-sculpture-can-stay-church-top-german-court-rules-2022-06-14/.

Schmitt, Carl. *Political Theology*. Translated by George Schwab. Cambridge, MA: MIT Press, 1985.

Spinoza, Benedict. *On the Improvement of the Understanding; The Ethics; Correspondence*. Translated by R. H. M. Elwes. 1883; repr., New York: Dover, 1955.

Tomba, Massimiliano. *Insurgent Universality: An Alternative Legacy of Modernity*. New York: Oxford University Press, 2019.

Wolin, Sheldon S. "Fugitive Democracy." *Constellations* 1, no. 1 (1994): 11–25. https://doi.org/10.1111/j.1467-8675.1994.tb00002.x.

Loren Goldman

Thomas Müntzer in the Marxist Imagination

ABSTRACT This essay explores Thomas Müntzer's polysemous reception in three classic works of Marxist historiography: Friedrich Engels's *Peasant War in Germany* (1850), Karl Kautsky's *Forerunners of Modern Socialism* (1895), and Ernst Bloch's *Thomas Müntzer as Theologian of the Revolution* (1921). All three studies track essentially the same events, but each author renders this past differently in light of their respective understandings of communism's contemporary challenges. Tracking the character of Müntzer in these accounts allows insight not only into the changing concerns of three successive generations of Marxists, but also into the ever-renewable actuality of history for the present.

KEYWORDS Thomas Müntzer, historiography, Ernst Bloch, Friedrich Engels, Karl Kautsky

On the five hundredth anniversary of his execution it is well worth inquiring into the function of Thomas Müntzer for the present. After all, Müntzer himself is and shall ever likely remain elusive. The impressive efforts of recent biographers notwithstanding (see, e.g., Goertz; Bräuer and Vogler; Drummond), we know little in detail about his life save for a few years toward its end; and the remarkable scholarship behind the recent critical edition of his work notwithstanding (Müntzer, *Thomas-Müntzer-Ausgabe*), Müntzer's writings are still incomplete and ambiguous, not to mention often corrupted. One of his best known, for example, the "Prague Protest"—commonly called the "Prague Manifesto" in a loaded echo of Marx and Engels—exists in four strikingly different versions, only two of which may be in Müntzer's hand, and the most comprehensive of which is likely in that of his notoriously careless amanuensis Ambrosius Emmen, leaving readers with the unfortunate possibility that some of his most celebrated recorded words may not in fact be his own.[1] This is not to say that Müntzer's work is mute: he unquestionably presents a radically egalitarian and politically charged alternative to the Lutheran doctrine of two kingdoms and the liberal quiescence that is its inheritance, and his everyman mysticism represents a full-throated rejection of top-

HISTORY of the PRESENT ▪ A Journal of Critical History ▪ 15:1 ▪ April 2025
DOI: 10.1215/21599785-11561509 © 2025 Duke University Press

down authority. Scandalous though his legacy may be in some regards, however, other aspects of his thought fly in the face of its assimilation to worldly politics; his strident apocalypticism, for example, arguably makes sense only in the Christian context of the supposed Last Days, and his Pauline aversion to sins of the flesh—he chided Melanchthon for endorsing conjugal sex, for example—fits poorly with interpretations, like Ernst Bloch's, that make him a prophet of earthly utopia. In short, the desultory circumstances of his life and work allow an unusually wide degree of interpretive latitude while at the same time throwing up obstacles to any simple or consistent reading.

The history of political thought unavoidably imposes fictive frames on the past in order to render it intelligible for the present, and thus there are always several theres there, as it were. Müntzer contains multitudes: radically democratic as well as radically otherworldly, driven to ameliorate suffering but also demanding that we suffer, aspirationally universalist yet sharply partisan, calling for the imitation of Christ while suggesting that membership in the elect does not require confessional Christianity. Divergent readers have selected aspects of his work in accordance with their pragmatic interests, emplotting him in narratives that express their own practical commitments (see Ricoeur, ch. 2; Dienstag; McManus; cf. White). In uses (and abuses) of Müntzer, one encounters not history as a simple representation of the past, but history intended to be memory, in Pierre Nora's words, "a perpetually active phenomenon, a bond tying us to the eternal present" that empowers acts going forward (Nora 8; Burke 59). One acts politically with or against the weight of history, and insofar as revolutionary moments promise a leap into the unknown, invoking precedents provides both reassurance and legitimation. Such appeals are common, even commonplace: the American framers draped themselves in Roman robes, just as Russian revolutionary populists, Bolsheviks, social revolutionaries, and anarchists alike fancied themselves inheritors of the French Commune, the French Revolution, and earlier Russian rebels.[2] It is no different in our case; indeed, Eric Hobsbawm (13) cites as an archetypal example of the invention of tradition Engels's *Peasant War in Germany*, the central protagonist of which is Müntzer.

This article accordingly focuses on how Müntzer gets differently interpellated in his three most influential Marxist treatments: Engels's *Peasant War in Germany* (1850), Karl Kautsky's *Forerunners of Modern Socialism* (1895), and Ernst Bloch's *Thomas Müntzer as Theologian of Revolution* (1921). While each of these thinkers sees Müntzer as a proto-communist, each also stresses qualities in him that reflect debates within their own respective generations of communist politics. Against the failings of conservative nationalism and the failure of the 1848 liberal revolution alike—movements for which Luther was taken as a patron saint of a united Germany—Engels offers an economic interpretation of the Reformation that elevates Müntzer to a left Hegelian *avant la lettre*, critical of religion and aspiring toward a proletarian universalism. Two generations later, against the backdrop of the German industrial revolution, Kautsky by contrast downplays Müntzer's agrarian bases and stresses his attempts to organize the early urban working class. Finally, against the scientific economism of dominant evolutionary socialism in his own day, Bloch focuses on Müntzer's activist millenarian theology as a model for bringing a new communist Jerusalem into being over the ruins of the Great War, and as further evidence for the actuality of his own central operator, the not-yet.

I jump directly into these thinkers' respective readings, forgoing further detailed treatment of the historiography of Müntzer and the Peasants' War, which has traditionally split into materialist and idealist camps. Some, that is, have stressed its economic and structural foundations, while others have stressed the centrality of its personal, ideological, and religious elements (for overviews, see Scribner; Midelfort; Scott, *Peasants' War* parts 1 and 2; Matheson, "Recent"; Müller, *Thomas Müntzer*; Müller, "Bauernkrieg"). Although this binary does not do justice to the richness of the scholarly literature on the topic, including the works by Engels, Kautsky, and Bloch, the latter all indeed prioritize a materialist perspective. At the same time, however, the diversity of their presentations shows that there is no single "Marxist" account of Müntzer's legacy, but a panoply of possibilities even within this radical frame.

Engels's *Peasant War in Germany*: Müntzer as Atheist Proto-communist

> The whole [revolution] in Germany will depend on whether it is possible to
> back the proletarian revolution by some second edition of The Peasant
> War. In that case the affair should go swimmingly.
> —Marx to Engels, April 16, 1856

Engels takes a long view that begins in 1476 with the Drummer of Niklashausen, "the first peasant conspiracy" (428), and ends with the battle of Frankenhausen in 1525. That Engels was drawn to the Peasants' War should not be surprising, for left Hegelians saw clear parallels between their own moment and Luther's day. Arnold Ruge wrote that "our life stands once again at the day of judgment, as it was with Christianity and the Reformation" (qtd. in Neher 74). Likewise, Wilhelm Zimmermann, Engels's principal historical source, wrote in 1844 that "the great movement of 1525 is intimately related to the recent aspirations and ferment, if not that of yesterday, but like the day before yesterday with that of today. The most meaningful sounds that pervade the present, are they not the same that rustled through the first decade of the Reformation? The same strings are being plucked, by one and the same spirit" (qtd. in Friesen, *Reformation* 9). Zimmermann meant his account to buttress nascent democratic and nationalist tendencies that eventually came to a head in the 1848 liberal revolution in Germany, when he himself was elected as a representative to the 1848–49 Frankfurt parliament (Friesen, "Wilhelm Zimmermann"). Under the influence of Eduard Gans, Zimmermann described the uprisings as an expression of the historical march of the spirit of freedom becoming more concretely manifest in the world. Müntzer is accordingly treated by Zimmermann as a more consistent harbinger of the bourgeois freedom that Luther had initially represented (Friesen, *Reformation* 129–30). Furthermore, he downplays Müntzer's theological commitments, seeing them, like Feuerbach, as merely the self-conscious expression of the human spirit, which finds its political form in a democratic revolution (Steinmetz 407–11; Friesen, *Reformation* 132). It is in contrast to this "highpoint of the bourgeois image of Müntzer" (Steinmetz 415) that Engels writes his account.

For Zimmermann, the French Revolution ushered in the new moment of democratic possibility, and Engels's famous claim that "the German people, too, have their revolutionary tradition" (399) is an attempt to match the prestige of that world-historical event. For Engels, the radical Reformation's failure was the result of the political fragmentation of the German people, not the weakness of the movement itself. Under different political circumstances, it would have "yielded the most magnificent results," for its "peasants and plebeians were full of ideas and plans that often make their descendants shudder" (399). Now the possibility is once again alive for the German people, albeit this time without the fragmentation of three centuries before. In seeking to "remind the German people of the clumsy yet powerful and tenacious figures of the German Peasant War," Engels hopes to show that its events are "not so impossibly far removed from our present struggle" in 1850. More pointedly, the opponents faced by the radical peasants and plebeians are "essentially the same," though "on a lower level of development" than those who communist revolutionaries now face: the bourgeoisie, who make possible yet fail to bring their democratizing revolution to its logical conclusion (399). Engels thus paints the past as prologue, positing that modern political institutions wrought by the recent nationalist upheaval can fulfill the promise first instantiated by the union of peasants and "plebeians" in the radical Reformation. The democratic revolution of 1848 may well have been, as Zimmermann has it, a culmination of sorts of Hegel's world-historical vision; the next and final stage of history, however, awaited the proletarian revolution (Friesen, *Reformation* 152). To put it in terms of Marx's "On the Jewish Question," political emancipation alone does not equal human emancipation; if 1848 approximated political emancipation, genuine human emancipation—from property, from religion, and from ideology—remains in the future. Engels's monograph makes the Peasants' War a dry run for the imminent revolution now in preparation thanks to ripened social, economic, and political conditions.

Like Marx later in *The Civil War in France*, Engels does not offer a reductive class account, but instead a messy, variegated, and striated portrait that includes the competing interests and power of the upper, middle, and lower nobility; a clergy stratified into various aristocratic and plebeian layers; and an array of other urban and rural patricians, burghers, artisans, and producers; and beneath it all, the exploited peasants. The division of society into two large camps so as to facilitate revolutionary transformation was "a rank impossibility," and "anything like it could only come about if the lowest stratum of the nation, the one exploited by all other estates, the peasants and the plebeians, would rise up" (410). And indeed, it was only "the embryonic proletarian element" of the plebeian faction in the towns—the "absolutely propertyless faction" (415) and "the only class that stood outside the existing official society" (414)—that were able to combine, "under the direct influence of Müntzer," with the thoroughly exploited peasantry to attain the self-consciousness necessary for it to be a potentially revolutionary class (408). For all of these muddled social dynamics, Engels sees the estates of sixteenth-century Germany as falling heuristically into three large camps whose struggle determined the course of the moment: "the Catholic or reactionary, the Lutheran bourgeois reformist, and the revolutionary" (411), represented by the established church, Luther and his followers, and Müntzer, respectively. The tale of the magisterial Reformation unfolds not as a theological battle, then, but as a material one (411-12), pitting bourgeois upstarts against the declining feudal status quo; likewise, the tale of the Peasants' War unfolds not on theological grounds, but as a material struggle of the embryonic proletariat and exploited lumpen peasantry against the ascendant bourgeoisie.

Thus Müntzer is for Engels not a religious figure but a political one (Friesen, *Reformation* 174–75; Vogler, "Die Entwicklung" 196; Vogler, *Müntzerbild* 110-13); indeed, he denies that Müntzer's theological claims are even rightly to be seen as religious. Zimmermann had emphasized Müntzer's appeals to mystical experience as a type of rational theology, and Engels follows him on this path. Having seen the failure of Luther to fulfill the promise of his democratizing reformation, Müntzer's "philosophical-theological doctrine attacked all the main points not only of Catholicism but of Christianity generally. . . . He preached a kind of pantheism, which curiously resembled modern speculative contemplation, and at times even approached atheism" insofar as "reason" alone justified faith (421). Müntzer accordingly becomes a political entrepreneur who brandishes religion as a weapon, well aware of Christianity as a human creation, maintaining the masquerade for masses too dense or weak to grasp this truth. Müntzer's activities thus had a "dual effect": "on the one hand, on the people, whom he addressed in the only language they could comprehend, that of religious prophecy; and on the other hand, on the initiated to whom he could disclose his ultimate aims" (426).

Although they come couched in apocalyptic language, Engels reads Müntzer's calls for a communalist ethic à la the early Church as a secular prophecy of the imminent communist future. When Müntzer called for the immediate establishment of the kingdom of God on earth, by this phrase he merely meant

> a society with no class differences, no private property and no state authority independent of, and foreign to, members of society. All the existing authorities, insofar as they refused to submit and join the revolution, were to be overthrown, all work and all property shared in common, and complete equality introduced. A union was to be established to realise all this, and not only throughout Germany, but throughout Christendom. Princes and lords would be invited to join, but should they refuse the union was to take up arms and overthrow or kill them at the first opportunity. (Engels 422)

In a move that similarly anticipates communism, Engels hears in Müntzer's call for the distribution of church lands not a complaint against confiscatory clerical lords, but a more general claim for the community of property (432). When, during his second sojourn in Mühlhausen, Müntzer finally had the opportunity to institute some of his revolutionary program, he failed because he was ahead of his time, with "little root in the then existing economic conditions" (470). Nor were the political conditions yet ripe for seeing such a revolutionary project through, as the inchoate German nation could not find unified voice given the fragmentation of its lands among myriad princes and lesser lords (480–81).[3]

Thus for Engels Müntzer is a visionary whose communist earthbound gaze anticipated a world that was not ready for realization. Through his efforts, the displaced plebeian townspeople made common cause with the exploited peasantry in a definite program of revolution; the revolution failed, but in the process its embryonic future agents gained consciousness of themselves as a unified, world-historical class. In the nineteenth century, more advanced conditions—the rise of industrial production and the consolidation of national governing institutions—meant that the preconditions for a successful revolution were in place, three hundred years after Müntzer had tried to first initiate it. The faltering nature of the liberal revolution put paid to Zimmermann's enlistment of the radical Reformation a few years earlier as a conceptual antecedent of the 1848–49 Frankfurt parliament to which he himself was elected; for Engels, by contrast, Müntzer's vision was not mystified by the tenuous promise of political representation, but instead perceived the need for a profound transformation in the economic structure of society if genuine emancipation were to be achieved. Furthermore, such a transformation could not be contained by national boundaries; in Müntzer's apocalyptic claim of the kingdom of God's imminent arrival, Engels saw the glimmers of a secularized universal communism of which German workers would be the spearhead and on whose cusp he and his contemporaries now stood.

Kautsky: Müntzer as Harbinger and Herald of the Urban Industrial Proletariat Class

If in 1850 Engels draws a direct line between Müntzer and contemporary global communism as a counter to Zimmermann's liberal nationalist embrace of Müntzer's legacy and in contrast to the reactionary nationalist embrace of Luther, forty-five years later, Kautsky homes in on Müntzer's appeal to the proto-industrial working class in contrast to the agrarian masses. Empirically, Kautsky does not go beyond what Engels presented; he acknowledged in a letter to the latter that he added nothing to Zimmermann's research and Engels's general materialist interpretation of history (B. Kautsky 423). He thus follows Engels and Zimmermann in his sketch of the economic and social circumstances of German-speaking lands on the verge of the revolution, noting the increasing immiseration of the peasantry despite the growing riches of the greater society, albeit with a heavy emphasis on the urban economic developments rather than the diversity and complexity of the countryside to which Engels was attuned (K. Kautsky, *Vorläufer* 8–11).[4] Like Engels, moreover, Kautsky notes that commerce and manufacturing had advanced most in Thüringia and Saxony, leaving them most ripe for antifeudal revolutionary political activity (25).

What is striking about Kautsky's treatment of Müntzer is how the aspects he does select reflect his own organizational and political preoccupations at the close of the nineteenth century, in contrast to the concerns Engels expressed in its middle. Engels and Kautsky were close—in their correspondence, Kautsky playfully called Engels "General" and Engels addressed Kautsky as

"Baron"—and Kautsky kept Engels abreast of his progress while writing his four-volume *Vorläufer des neueren Sozialismus* (*Forerunners of Modern Socialism*). After learning of the project, Engels reminded Kautsky of the importance of telling the story of the Reformation "from *our* standpoint, how much [it] was a directly necessary *bourgeois* movement" (B. Kautsky 328). And so Kautsky does, albeit being more cavalier in his use of his contemporary referential frame. Where Engels peppers his text with phrases describing various constellations of forces in the Reformation as "exactly the same" or "essentially the same" as those in his present, he still maintains a sense of historical remove and takes care to speak of sixteenth-century precedents as embryonic forms or anticipations of the nineteenth century. Kautsky (*Vorläufer*) exhibits little such caution, referring to the magisterial opposition to the princes simply as "bourgeois" and the plebeian opposition as "communist" (30), and describing Müntzer not as anticipating communism but simply as "the center of the entire communist movement in Germany" (41) from 1521 to 1525, as well as "the most brilliant embodiment of rebellious, heretical communism" (122). Kautsky also significantly simplifies the class character of the age (62), with special emphasis on urban workers at the expense of the peasantry (Friesen, *Reformation* 173), not to mention a pronounced stress on mining and metallurgy, the sectors to which he had dedicated an earlier article that was his first engagement with Müntzer (K. Kautsky, "Die Bergarbeiter"). Thus although Engels writes to Kautsky that many aspects of the latter's treatment of Müntzer and the period as a whole improve on his own, he also chides Kautsky for anachronistically referring to sixteenth-century weavers and miners as "proletariats" rather than "pre-proletariats" (B. Kautsky 435). And while Kautsky (*Vorläufer*) offers that Müntzer's uprising was "interlocal," "only one link in a long chain of revolutionary uprisings, whose collective effect would be to kill tyranny and exploitation" (96), Engels also complains that Kautsky's more detailed exposition of proto-capitalist industries and commerce in Saxony and Thüringia was inadequately contextualized within the greater dynamics of nascent capitalism as an international economic system (B. Kautsky 435; cf. Kautsky's response, 438–43).

In response, Kaustky explains that, unlike Engels, he had read Müntzer's texts closely (B. Kautsky 328–29), an experience that brought him to different conclusions. First, while Kautsky treats Christianity "only as a *would be* communist organization, as a church, not as *Weltanschauung*" (B. Kautsky 405; "would be" written in English), rather than characterizing Müntzer as a rational theologian-cum-atheist, full stop, he describes him as a "pantheistic mystic" (K. Kautsky, *Vorläufer* 55). This makes Müntzer for him no less of a practical and politically minded figure, however, for he tells Engels that he considers chiliasm not something otherworldly but rather "most earthly" (B. Kautsky 406). Another difference is Kautsky's (*Vorläufer*) contention that Müntzer surpassed his "communist comrades" not because of his "philosophical sense" or "organizational talent" but by dint of his "revolutionary vigor" and "above all, his statesmanlike vision" (46). While Engels mildly engages Müntzer's theology and his embryonic world-historical significance, Kautsky is far more taken with his tactics. "Other communists of the middle ages were . . . of a generally pacifistic nature," a characteristic from which the extraordinarily violent Müntzer was "far removed." He understood that the existing power relations in state and society would not fall to weapons like ideas and the holy spirit, and chose to meet their violence "with all his mystical enthusiasm" (46). Müntzer threatened the deeply rooted conditions of an exploitative society, and his failure wasn't because of the weakness of his ideas or the unpreparedness of society for his innovations as such, but because he could not muster the force to transform his world thoroughly enough. In contrast to Engels, and notwithstanding the title of his work, Kautsky makes Müntzer less of a forerunner than a contemporary, changing his motley coalition of farmers and townspeople into an industrial working class in search of the appropriate means of obtaining political power. From a later vantage point than Engels, moreover, Kautsky is able to add another link to the long chain of revolutionary correlates stretching back to the assorted "communists" of the sixteenth century, noting that Müntzer's uprising in Mühlhausen on March 18, 1525, shares the date with both the 1848 Berlin revolution and the 1871 Paris Commune.

Although Kautsky thus rides very much in Engels's wake, his presentation is differently inflected by the structural transformations over the half century separating their accounts as well as his own vocation as a theorist of a mass political party. His understanding of the societal cleavages in Müntzer's world flattens Engels's more stratified social topography, reflecting the basic division between capitalists and workers Kautsky perceived in a Germany that had since industrialized, and rendering actual the socioeconomic conditions that Engels had earlier considered only nascent during the Reformation. Müntzer's universalist edge is also subdued; the 1870 unification of Germany meant that for practical purposes Kautsky's political energies were now concentrated on organizing within the legal framework of a now existing state potentially amenable to transformation from within through democratic participation. While Müntzer remains an ideologist of the kingdom of God for Kautsky, he nonetheless foregrounds the kingdom itself, lauding Müntzer in particular for his tactical sense as a statesman of class consciousness. And while the Peasants' War raged across a broad swath of the

unpropertied populace, Kautsky's reformer leads with the weavers and especially the miners, predecessors of the industrial, urban proletariat that
embodied the core constituency of his own Social Democratic Party.

Bloch: Müntzer, a Lenin of the Apocalypse

Bloch's take on Müntzer is often assimilated to Engels's materialist account
(e.g., Vogler, *Müntzerbild* 110–13), yet this perspective ignores the fundamentally different nature of Bloch's idiosyncratic intellectual project, namely, to
secure the place of utopia within Marxism. Bloch's differences with Engels
and other strict materialists are evident in his title, *Thomas Müntzer as Theologian of Revolution*: he treats Müntzer first and foremost as a religious
thinker. Bloch's idiosyncratic approach is also clear from his book's opening
chapter, which begins with the claim that "we always want to simply be with
ourselves," an appeal to Hegel's notion of freedom as being "with oneself" or,
better yet, "at home" (*bei sich*), later used by Marx to express the absence of
alienation. Bloch accordingly presents Müntzer tendentiously, not in any
pejorative sense, but in the sense of drawing out what immanent tendencies
in Müntzer speak to the present moment, rather than aiming for a scientific
or antiquarian history that shows only what actually happened, full stop. If
one insists on Rankean objectivity, Bloch's account may indeed be bad history, but from his side it is an acknowledgment that such objective history is
unrealistically motivated, an ethereal and even cold practice that is essentially utopian in its literal sense. In other words, Bloch treats Müntzer *as if* he
were a proto-communist, which is not the same as the naive and ahistorical
claim (voiced by Kautsky, for example) that he *was* a communist in any relevant contemporary sense. Bloch accordingly writes that "we don't really
look backwards, but always vitally mix ourselves in. . . . The dead return
to life, their deeds are with us once again." Müntzer, that is, along with
"his and all past events worth recording are therefore there in order to com-
pel and inspire us, to sustain us all the more in that which is eternally
intended-for-us" (9). Müntzer is one figure in a great repository of utopian
appearances whose actuality is ever present as a promise of what may yet
arrive.

Bloch offers largely the same set of historical facts about Müntzer's context as one finds in Zimmermann, Engels, and Kautsky, three of his main
sources. The peasants are defenseless and exploited (53), new manufacturing
relations are developing thanks to capital (51), and the miners are especially
restive—a point he takes from Kautsky (*Vorläufer* 41, 108). Numerous uprisings, as the others also note, precede the great conflagration associated
with Müntzer (53–54). Yet unlike his predecessors, each of whom discusses

Müntzer within longer accounts of the Peasants' War, Bloch focuses almost exclusively on Müntzer himself, taking his liberation theology as exemplary of the fantasy of utopian rupture that Bloch held indispensable for any radical politics, and personalizing the revolution in line with his own veneration of Lenin as an avatar of revolutionary action. As a result, Bloch cannot but emphasize Müntzer's chiliasm and throws himself into both the letter and spirit of Müntzer's texts along with their aftereffects on subsequent religion and philosophy.

What Bloch does bring to the facts is a heightened sensitivity to the complexity of historical causality. Economic appetite matters, without question, and yet it is "not the sole, not the persistently strongest, nor the most idiosyncratic motive of the human soul, especially in religiously charged times" (*Thomas Müntzer* 55). As such, "the purely economic perspective does not alone suffice to fully, utterly conditionally, or causally explain even the *appearance* of an historical event as important as the Peasants' War, not to mention the fact that such an analysis would risk dissolving the deeper *substance* of the human history glowing here" (55), namely, the "conscious dream" of a better world that pulls us forward. In this regard, Bloch reveals his unorthodoxy, *pace* Engels and Kautsky, in seeing the Peasants' War as inextricably connected to aspirations that cannot be merely reduced to a mystifying ideological product: "The original essential element itself must be considered all the more in addition to the economically existing elements of its precipitation and the conflict's content: as an activity of the most ancient dream, as the broadest outbreak in the history of heretics, as the ecstasy of the upright gait and of the impatient, rebellious, most serious will to paradise" (56).[5] Müntzer's "great economic-historical insight" is, moreover, quite real (47). The reason he found himself at the center of the rebellion is that he was not only a political talisman and a representative of an embryonic proletariat but also a theologian and, most importantly, because he fervently embodied the fundamental human yearning for utopia, a Pentecost of the not-yet. Initially in the garb of a Lutheran, Müntzer soon reveals himself to be "a class-conscious, revolutionary, chiliastic communist" (25). The content of his teachings distinguished Müntzer from the magisterial reformers, but what truly set him apart was his "sense of mission" in contrast to "Luther's paradoxical servility" (32). This consciousness is inseparable from his chiliasm and distinct from the ultimately contingent class consciousness Engels and Kautsky see as Müntzer's main legacy. Indeed, this chiliasm, misguided though it may be in its particulars from an orthodox perspective, gave form to a concretely revolutionary disposition despite itself. That is to say that for Bloch, Müntzer's value inheres not in his proto-communist immanence but rather in his transcendence, for in seeking to overshoot the earthly he ultimately drew those who followed him closer to the real possibility of bringing heaven down to earth; he is a living representative of the "warm stream" of passionate striving in contrast to the "cold stream" of sober analysis (*Principle* 1: 208). At the same time, like all great utopian exemplars for Bloch, Müntzer "only more broadly shaped what was already alive long before" (*Thomas Münzer* 103). Put another way, despite Müntzer's evident Christian enthusiasm, his ultimate value for Bloch is as a prophet of what he later called "transcending without any heavenly transcendence" (*Principle* 3: 1288; cf. *Atheism*).

Looking forward, Bloch concludes that Müntzer provides a model in gross for the coming (metaphorical) kingdom of God on earth:

> Now, fully matured, the heirs of Müntzer's weavers and clothmakers stand on the revolutionary plan, no longer to be driven off. The era walks upright under their burden, their mission; the final socially possible class, heir of the peasantry, the tangential force that tears them away into eternity, is being liberated, the explosion of the principle of class and the principle of power, the final earthly revolution is being born. (*Thomas Münzer* 110)

"The portentous manifesto of the Red German Forty-Eighters shines high above once more," he writes, welcoming this moment when "the true spirit of the Reformation is awakening" and a renewed apocalyptic sensibility "finally creates the path out of the old world, power, and ground toward the final myth, toward absolute transformation" (110). While this old world lies in ruins—Bloch commenced his Müntzer work in the immediate aftermath of the Great War—the spirit of genuine utopia nevertheless shines over its shattered ruins (229), illuminating the horizon and remaining visible to those willing to look inside themselves.

Ultimately, and unlike Engels and Kautsky, Bloch takes Müntzer as a model for both his mysticism and the urgency of his call. The mysticism is appealing insofar as it connects our innermost desires with a push for outer emancipation. By focusing our gaze inward, Müntzer turns us "toward the clearing of our own lived instant itself, toward the adequation of our wonder, our premonition, our persistent and profoundest dream of bliss, truth, disenchantment of ourselves, of secret divinity and glory" (228), in line with Bloch's philosophical anthropology of anticipatory consciousness. We only want to be with ourselves, that is, but within ourselves we find the immanent aspiration toward utopia. Introspection does not become otherworldly, but focuses our vision on an immanent (and imminent) future in which our ostensibly deepest yearning can be actualized in reality. Müntzer shows that the liberation of the authentic self, properly understood, entails earthly action, a breaking of the bonds of the given, of quiescence to the way things are rather than the way things can and must become. For Bloch, the ultimate message of Müntzer's asceticism is not a refusal of the world tout court, but a refusal of a world fundamentally hostile to real human flourishing.

Accordingly, rather than shy away from Müntzer's Last Days apocalypticism, Bloch reads it as the cry of the oppressed for a new world. The lived instant of any moment promises the possibility of rupture: the term *Durchbruch* ("breakthrough") pervades *Thomas Münzer als Theologe der Revolution*. The second and central lesson of Müntzer for Bloch is thus his revolutionary insistence on hastening the apocalypse's arrival. In this regard, in heralding a religious dawn, Müntzer is a harbinger of a Marxist philosophy of praxis rooted in the recognition that—to cite Karl Korsch (95)—"theoretical criticism and practical overthrow are here inseparable activities." His apocalypticism amounts to a call for revolutionary action, in which every moment contains the "presence of the now," in Bloch's friend Walter Benjamin's (205) famous phrase, and which holds the promise of "blast[ing] a specific era out of the homogenous course of history" (207). For Bloch, Müntzer is thus an archetypal thinker of what Benjamin would later, in an essay marked by the influence of Bloch's Müntzer book, describe as "Messianic time" (208), the eternal now in which humans working in concert could seize the initiative and usher in utopia. In 1921 Bloch saw Müntzer in Lenin, or rather Lenin in Müntzer, a visionary who calls for us, together, to build a concrete bridge between reality and utopia, pointing to revolution as the process of drawing out of ourselves the future we are and have always already been seeking.

Conclusion: Müntzer as History and Actuality

Müntzer's actuality is not merely a function of his insurgency against the ruling powers of his day, but also the fact that the very elusiveness of his work and presence allows him to be malleably interpellated. It is for good reason that radicals have embraced him, for he is that rare historical figure who posed both a conceptual and practical threat to privileged orders for the sake of the common man. And yet precisely because the actual Müntzer is lost in the mists of time, it is possible and even necessary to contemporize him.

Bloch writes in *The Principle of Hope* that thinking means to go beyond or to overstep (1: 5). To think Müntzer in the present—and in any moment—requires going beyond his fragmentary remains. While schematizing him as a proto-communist is tendentious (as Friedemann Stengel notes, the only account of his famous *omnia sunt communia* comes in a report of his supposed confession under torture), it also reflects undeniable *tendencies* in his thought, a plausible latent subtext for the effective realization of an earthly kingdom of God on the model of a metaphysically transcendent kingdom in heaven that knows neither class nor confession.

Müntzer's radical legacy, however, is neither as simple nor monochromatic as standard accounts have it (see Steinmetz; Friesen, *Reformation*; Vogler, *Müntzerbild*). My foray into Marxist appropriations of him reveals a variety of different ends-in-view to which his figure was applied. Engels pioneered Müntzer's radical reception by making him a secular communist nationalist-cum-internationalist against the liberal nationalist antecedent Zimmermann had seen; Kautsky rendered him a predecessor of his own organizational efforts among the urban proletariat; Bloch found a prophet of a utopia that has not yet arrived but which stands at the door if we are bold enough to embrace it. Liberation theologians attended to his religious appeals to both the materially and spiritually poor, while rebels in Chiapas localized and indigenized his call for the self-government of the commons (Zorzin 86–88). Each made Müntzer legible as an ally in their respective projects, reflecting the changing circumstances of their contemporary battles. It is for good reason that Massimiliano Tomba enlists Müntzer as an exemplar of "insurgent universality" (26) an underground current of thinking that calls for revolutionary rupture with present orders of power, such that the sedimented layers of historical time get broken apart and "anachronistic elements are reconfigured in an original way" (10). Müntzer's varied appearance even within the relatively unified Marxist frame is a reminder, however, that his figure—like that of any historical character—also unavoidably reflects the insurgent particularity of those who summon it. ∎

Loren Goldman is associate professor in political science at the University of Pennsylvania. He is the author of *The Principle of Political Hope* (2023), cotranslator of Ernst Bloch's *Avicenna and the Aristotelian Left* (2019), and is currently translating Bloch's *Thomas Müntzer as Theologian of Revolution* (2025).

ACKNOWLEDGMENTS

For helpful comments or other assistance, I thank Michael Baylor, Terrell Carver, Chris Chambers, Charles Cobine, Andy Drummond, Judith Grant, Margrit Apollonia Jay (RIP), Joel T. Luber, Thomas T. Müller, Anne Norton, Niklas Plaetzer, Avshalom Schwartz, Joan Scott, Matt Shafer, Max Tomba, and the editors of *History of the Present*. This article is dedicated to Ellen Kennedy.

NOTES

1   A state of affairs captured by the fact that Michael Baylor reasonably translates Müntzer's insulting description of Luther as *eselfortzig* as both "donkey-fart" (Baylor,

Radical) and the more arresting "donkey-cunt" (Müntzer, "Sermon to the Princes" 13; also Baylor, *Revelation*). Indeed, even Ingo Warnke's (130) detailed dictionary of Müntzer's word usage often remains speculative (incidentally, his anodyne rendering of *eselfortzig* is simply "asinine" [*eselig*]).

2   See, e.g., Arshinov 144–45; Avrich 122, 264–66; Bailyn ch. 2; Depretto; Deutscher; Figes and Kolonitskii ch. 2; Kondratieva; Shlapentokh, *French*; Shlapentokh, *Counter*; Tchoudinov; Wood ch. 2.

3   Given what Engels says about the instrumentality of Müntzer's prophetic language, his brief in favor of nationalism—his reading of Luther's and Müntzer's push for vernacular liturgy as an instrumental proto-nationalism rather than a genuine desire to have Christians "know" God more effectively, for example—may suggest a similar tactical use of a common conceptual vernacular rather than something that he himself held strongly. He follows Zimmermann in claiming that the German red-gold-black tricolor was the banner of the peasant union (446); the peasants held many different banners, but none apparently were the modern German tricolor.

4   An abridged version of the Kautsky chapters discussed here was published in 1897 under the title *Communism in Central Europe in the Time of the Reformation*; all references are to the 1921 German edition and are my own translations.

5   In his afterword to the revised edition, Bloch (*Thomas Müntzer* 230) describes his book as a "coda" to *The Spirit of Utopia* (1918), the product of "revolutionary romanticism" later moderated by the materialism of *The Principle of Hope* (1954–59).

WORKS CITED

Arshinov, Peter. *History of the Makhnovist Movement, 1918–1921*. Detroit: Black and Red, 1974.

Avrich, Paul. *Russian Rebels*. New York: Norton, 1976.

Bailyn, Bernard. *The Ideological Origins of the American Revolution*. Cambridge, MA: Harvard Belknap Press, 1992.

Baylor, Michael, ed. and trans. *The Radical Reformation*. Cambridge: Cambridge University Press, 1991.

Baylor, Michael, ed. and trans. *Revelation and Revolution: The Basic Writings of Thomas Müntzer*. Bethlehem, PA: Lehigh University Press, 1993.

Benjamin, Walter. "Theses on the Philosophy of History." In *Illuminations*, edited by Hannah Arendt, 196–209. Boston: Mariner, 2019.

Bloch, Ernst. *Atheism in Christianity: The Religion of Exodus and the Kingdom*. Translated by J. T. Swann. London: Verso, 2009.

Bloch, Ernst. *The Principle of Hope*. Translated by Neville Plaice, Stephen Plaice, and Paul Knight. 3 vols. Cambridge, MA: MIT Press, 1986.

Bloch, Ernst. *Thomas Münzer als Theologe der Revolution*. Vol. 2, *Ernst Bloch Gesamtausgabe*. Frankfurt: Surhkamp, 1977.

Bräuer, Siegfried, and Günter Vogler. *Thomas Müntzer: Neu Ordnung machen in der Welt*. Gütersloh: Gütersloher Verlagshaus, 2016.

Burke, Peter. *Varieties of Cultural History*. Ithaca, NY: Cornell University Press, 1997.

Depretto, Catherine. "Révolution française de 1789 contre temps des troubles russe: Paradigmes de lecture de 1917." *Revue des études slaves* 90, nos. 1–2 (2019): 141–52.

Deutscher, Isaac. "The French Revolution and the Russian Revolution: Some Suggestive Analogies." *World Politics* 4, no. 3 (1952): 369–81.

Dienstag, Joshua Foa. *Dancing in Chains: Narrative and Memory in Political Theory*. Palo Alto, CA: Stanford University Press, 1997.

Drummond, Andrew. *The Dreadful History and Judgement of God on Thomas Müntzer: The Life and Times of an Early German Revolutionary*. London: Verso, 2024.

Engels, Frederick. *The Peasant War in Germany*. In *1849–51*, vol. 10 of *Karl Marx and Frederick Engels, Collected Works*, 397–482. New York: International Publishers, 1978.

Figes, Orlando, and Boris Kolonitskii. *Interpreting the Russian Revolution: The Language and Symbols of 1917*. New Haven, CT: Yale University Press, 1999.

Friesen, Abraham. *Reformation and Utopia: The Marxist Interpretation of the Reformation and Its Antecedents*. Wiesbaden: Franz Steiner Verlag, 1974.

Friesen, Abraham. "Wilhelm Zimmermann and the Nemesis of History." *German Studies Review* 4, no. 2 (1981): 195–236.

Goertz, Hans-Jürgen. *Thomas Müntzer: Revolutionär am Ende der Zeiten*. Munich: C. H. Beck, 2015.

Hobsbawm, Eric. "Introduction: Inventing Traditions." In *The Invention of Tradition*, edited by Eric Hobsbawm and Terence Ranger, 1–14. Cambridge: Cambridge University Press, 2012.

Kautsky, Benedikt, ed. *Friedrich Engels' Briefwechsel mit Karl Kautsky*. Vienna: Danubia-Verlag, 1955.

Kautsky, Karl. *Communism in Central Europe in the Time of the Reformation*. Translated by J. L. and E. G. Mulliken. London: Fisher and Unwin, 1897.

Kautsky, Karl. "Die Bergarbeiter und der Bauernkrieg." *Die Neue Zeit* 7 (1889): 289–97, 337–50, 410–17, 443–53, 507–15.

Kautsky, Karl. *Vorläufer des neueren Sozialismus*. Vol. 4. Stuttgart: J. H. W. Dietz, 1921.

Kondratieva, Tamara. "La fin du révolutions: Raskol'nikov et Robespierre." *Cahiers du monde Russe* 58, nos. 1–2 (2017): 147–78.

Korsch, Karl. *Marxism and Philosophy*. Translated by Fred Halliday. London: Verso, 2012.

Marx, Karl, and Friedrich Engels. *Letters 1856–1859*. Vol. 40 of *Collected Works*. New York: International Publishers, 1983.

Matheson, Peter, ed. *The Collected Works of Thomas Müntzer*. Edinburgh: T & T Clark, 1988.

Matheson, Peter. "Recent German Research on Thomas Müntzer." *Mennonite Quarterly Review* 86, no. 1 (2012): 97–109.

McManus, Susan. *Fictive Theories*. London: Palgrave, 2005.

Midelfort, H. C. Erik. "The Revolution of 1525? Recent Studies of the Peasants' War." *Central European History* 11, no. 2 (1978): 189–206.

Müller, Thomas T. "Bauernkrieg in Thüringen: Eine kurze rezeptionsgeschichtliche Einführung." In *Reformation und Bauernkrieg*, edited by Werner Greiling, Thomas T. Müller, and Uwe Schirmer, 9–17. Wien: Böhlau Verlag, 2018.

Müller, Thomas T. *Thomas Müntzer im Bauernkrieg: Fakten-Fiktionen-Desiderate*. Mühlhausen, Germany: Thomas-Müntzer-Gesellschaft, 2016.

Müntzer, Thomas. "Sermon to the Princes." In *Wu Ming Presents Thomas Müntzer: Sermon to the Princes*, 12–35. Translated by Michael Baylor. London: Verso, 2010.

Müntzer, Thomas. *Thomas-Müntzer-Ausgabe: Kritische Gesamtausgabe*. 3 vols. Edited by Helmar Junghans and Armin Kohnle. Leipzig: Sächsische Akademie der Wissenschaften.

Neher, Walter. *Arnold Ruge als Politiker und politischer Schriftsteller: Ein Beitrag zur deutschen Geschichte des 19. Jahrhunderts*. Heidelberg, Germany: Carl Winters Universitätsbuchhandlung, 1933.

Nora, Pierre. "Between Memory and History: Les Lieux de Mémoire." *Representations* 26 (Spring 1989): 7–24.

Ricoeur, Paul. *Time and Narrative*. Translated by Kathleen McLaughlin and David Pellauer. Vol. 1. Chicago: University of Chicago Press, 1984.

Scott, Tom. "The Peasants' War: A Historiographical Review: Part One." *Historical Journal* 22, no. 3 (1979): 693–720.

Scott, Tom. "The Peasants' War: A Historiographical Review: Part Two." *Historical Journal* 22, no. 4 (1979): 953–74.

Scribner, Bob. "Is There a Social History of the Reformation?" *Social History* 2, no. 4 (1977): 483–505.

Shlapentokh, Dmitry. *The Counter-revolution in Revolution: Images of Thermidor and Napoleon at the Time of Russian Revolution and Civil War*. New York: St. Martin's, 1999.

Shlapentokh, Dmitry. *The French Revolution in Russian Intellectual Life, 1865–1905*. Westport, CT: Praeger, 1996.

Steinmetz, Max. *Das Müntzerbild von Martin Luther Bis Friedrich Engels*. Berlin: VEB Deutscher Verlag der Wissenschaften, 1971.

Stengel, Friedemann. "*Omnia sunt communia:* Gütergemeinschaft bei Müntzer?" *Archiv für Reformationsgeschichte* 102, no. 1 (2011): 133–74.

Tchoudinov, Alexandre V. "Le Culte Russe de la Révolution Francaise." *Cahiers du monde Russe* 48, nos. 2–3 (2007): 485–98.

Tomba, Massimiliano. *Insurgent Universality: An Alternative Legacy of Modernity*. Oxford: Oxford University Press, 2019.

Vogler, Günter. "Die Entwicklung eines marxistischen Müntzerbildes: Positionen, Probleme, Perspektiven." *Die Zeichen der Zeit* 43, nos. 7–8 (1989): 195–98.

Vogler, Günter. *Müntzerbild und Müntzerforschung vom 16. Bis zum 21. Jahrhundert, Band 2: 1789 bis 2017*. Berlin: Weidler Buchverlag, 2021.

Warnke, Ingo. *Wörterbuch zu Thomas Müntzers deutschen Schriften und Briefen*. Berlin: De Gruyter, 2017.

White, Hayden. *Metahistory: The Historical Imagination in Nineteenth-Century Europe*. 40th anniversary ed. Baltimore, MD: Johns Hopkins University Press, 2014.

Wood, Gordon. *The Idea of America*. New York: Penguin, 2011.

Zorzin, Alejandro. "Thomas Müntzer, in Latin America." *History of the Present* 15, no. 1 (2025): 72–92.

Alejandro Zorzin

TRANSLATED BY LOREN GOLDMAN

Thomas Müntzer, in Latin America

ABSTRACT This article offers a history of the reception of Thomas Müntzer's theology in Latin America. In this context, Müntzer has been seen primarily through the lens of his influential Marxist readers, particularly Friedrich Engels and Ernst Bloch. This legacy allows a direct line to be drawn from Müntzer to both liberation theology and the peasant rebellion in Chiapas.

KEYWORDS Thomas Müntzer, liberation theology, Anabaptism, German Peasants' War, Latin America

1. Spanish Translations of Friedrich Engels and Ernst Bloch

To this day, the reception of Thomas Müntzer in all of Latin America is defined by the work of Friedrich Engels's *German Peasants' War* and Ernst Bloch's *Thomas Müntzer as Theologian of Revolution*.

The first Spanish translation of Engels appeared in 1946 in Argentina; another edition was printed in 1970. In his introduction to the latter edition, the editor, L. Paz, described it as a classic work that could not be ignored: "Any study related to the German sixteenth century must acknowledge it; disregarding it is an unjustifiable omission" (Engels, *Las guerras campesinas* 7). The appendix to this edition also includes a Spanish translation of the *Twelve Articles of the Swabian Peasants*, for they, according to the editor, "are as good as unknown to Spanish speaking readers" (7). An early 1989 statement by the Brazilian liberation theologian Carlos Alberto Libânio Christo O. P. ("Frei Betto") confirms the influence of Engels's *German Peasants' War* in the Ibero-American context. In response to an interlocutor's comment that one of the most popular "absolute truths" of Marxism is the identification of religion as the opium of the people, Frei Betto answered that Engels spoke quite positively about religion when, for example, he examined the relationship be-

HISTORY of the PRESENT ▪ A Journal of Critical History ▪ 15:1 ▪ April 2025
DOI: 10.1215/21599785-11561520 © 2025 Duke University Press

tween the peasant conflicts in sixteenth-century Germany and the peasants' Christian beliefs. "When [Engels] analyses the peasant struggle of Thomas Müntzer, he speaks positively of religion as a factor of political emulation among the peasants" (Betto, "Debate").

In 1964 Ernst Bloch's *Thomas Münzer, théologien de la revolution* was published by Editions Juillard in Paris in an annotated translation by Maurice de Gandillac with a foreword by Rosemary Ferencz. On the basis of this French edition and the German original, Jorge Deike Robles translated the work into Spanish for the Madrid press Ciencia Nueva. This translation appeared under the title *Thomas Münzer, teólogo de la revolución*. Despite numerous interventions by the Franco regime's censors,[1] this Spanish Bloch edition became available in 1968 for Latin American readers. In 1973 an Ibero-American edition of Bloch's Müntzer book appeared in Rio de Janeiro in a Brazilian-Portuguese translation by Vamireh Chacon and Celeste Aída Galeão. In terms of the history of its reception and influence, it is significant that Bloch's Müntzer book was discussed at an early 1967 colloquium organized by the Centro Internacional de Documentación (Cuernavaca, Mexico) on "Violence, Imagination, and Social Change in Latin America."

2. Ibero-American Works on Thomas Müntzer (1970–2006)

The first Ibero-American work on Thomas Müntzer appeared in 1970, in the *Revista de teología*, a journal published since 1954 by the Missouri Lutheran Church in Buenos Aires.[2] Under the title "The Theology of Revolution and Thomas Müntzer," its rector Federico Lange primarily argued, with strongly polemical overtones, against the positions of the Presbyterian Richard Shaull[3] (yet which he had not connected to Müntzer), a lecturer in Brazil until 1964.[4] Lange starts from the assumption that "the theology of revolution rejects the doctrine of two kingdoms, and thus T. Muenzer [*sic*] is praised to the detriment of M. Luther." Müntzer is then only briefly presented on the basis of citations in Roland H. Bainton's (1955) book on Luther. The general thrust follows Ulrich Asendorf's 1969 article "The Doctrine of Two Kingdoms and the Theology of Revolution," which appeared in *Jahrbuch des Martin Luther Bundes*.

In the context of this debate, a second article on Müntzer appeared at the end of 1971 in the *Cuadernos de teología*. With the title "A Utopian Encounter," Manfred Bahmann, an ethnically German, North American Lutheran lecturer at the Facultad Luterana de Teología (in José C. Paz city, Buenos Aires Province), fashioned a fictional conversation between Luther and Müntzer. According to Bahmann, it "could have taken place in heaven, hell, purgatory, or anywhere else" (53). Using excerpts from Müntzer's "Vindication and Refutation" and Luther's "Open Letter on the Harsh Book against the

Peasants," these eight pages offer a pointed confrontation of the positions of both reformers in the "critical years of the peasants' rebellion in Germany" (53). Bahmann's original work, the first to convey in Spanish longer quotes from primary sources, clarifies two issues that continue to characterize the Ibero-American Müntzer reception:

1. The location of works on Müntzer within the context of greater evangelical church academic institutions in South and Central America (e.g., Instituto Superior Evangélico de Estudios Teológicos (ISEDET) in Buenos Aires, Argentina; Escola Superior de Teología in São Leopoldo, Brasil; and Seminario Bíblico Latinamericano in San José de Costa Rica);

2. The lack of possibility of directly engaging with Müntzer's writings in either Spanish or Brazilian Portuguese.

In 1970–71, the Mennonite theologian John Howard Yoder was a guest lecturer at the ISEDET and the Mennonite seminary (in Montevideo). A lasting and important result of his activities in the Río de la Plata was his groundbreaking compilation and annotation of sources under the title *Textos escogidos de la Reforma radical*, first published in 1976 in a Spanish translation by Nélida Meilaharzu de Machain and Ernesto Suárez Vilela in Buenos Aires. That collection made available for the first time to a wider Ibero-American public (two thousand copies) Spanish versions of a number of works: Müntzer's "Sermon to the Princes"; his letters to Frederick the Wise (October 4, 1523), to the People of Allstedt (April 1525), and to Count Albrecht and Count Ernst of Mansfeld (May 12, 1525); as well as the letter of Conrad Grebel and his Zurich companions to Müntzer (September 5, 1524). Regarding his criteria for selection, Yoder writes:

> We have given priority to the most readable and translatable works. Many of the most significant texts for the historical development of doctrine are difficult to interpret. This is related to their rich metaphorical language, their at times obscure biblical and contemporary allusions, their aberrant literary style and singular word usage, and also the complexity or even confusion of their trains of thought. (32)[5]

According to Yoder, what characterizes Müntzer's message is "the particular link between his very interiorized mysticism and the hope for a social revolution. All the same, he had no subversive intentions, for he expected that the princes would let themselves be made tools of the impending transformation stipulated by God" (17).

Yoder, who is not disparagingly critical of Müntzer, holds that it is fruitless to search for a link that "unites the mystic and the agitator"

(98), and the connection between both aspects of his thought can most likely be worked out if the "unity of the man Müntzer" is assumed and an attempt is made to

interpret his vision of revolution from the perspective of his spiritualism. The purpose of imminent divine intervention—be it with the aid of the Turks, the princes, or the people against the princes—is not the establishment of a new society, but a new spirituality. It is evident that [for Müntzer] the godless who have no right to live are not the exploitative princes, but rather the monks, priests, and scribes who obscure the way of true faith from common people. The absence of any utopian vision or detailed description of a new order is also evident; killing the godless is sufficient—God will do the rest. (98)

In addition, Yoder holds that not all scholars agree about "whether Thomas Müntzer held a social theory in the sense that he imagined models of just structures, had a normative vision, a utopia." Müntzer's "conviction with regard to the apocalyptic quality of social movement" is nonetheless clear. This aspect of his thought is, however, not reflected in his printed pamphlets, for they are related to his "theological and personal campaign against Luther." For that, one must draw from Müntzer's letters (121).

In the middle of the 1970s, then, Yoder had provided a solid foundation for an Ibero-American engagement with Müntzer. In the preface to Yoder's compilation and commentary, the Argentinian theologian José Míguez Bonino (lecturer in systematic theology at the ISEDET) writes,

The texts of the radical reformation can have fruitful potential for the theological renewal that has begun on our continent. . . . A contemporary historian, rooted in the same tradition, now makes it possible for us to situate it historically. But the hermeneutic circle will only be completed with a Latin American reading of these texts, a reading that emanates from the crisis of our own history, the experience and commitment of our own faith. (5)

As to the question of why this foundation did not have a greater impact at the time, it should be recognized that throughout the 1960s political power was in the hands of military regimes whose strict censorship measures made scholarship on "revolutionary" guiding principles extremely difficult in most of South and Central America. Military governments were installed first in Brazil in April 1964 (growing increasingly oppressive beginning in 1968 [see, e.g., Betto, *Batismo*]); beginning in July 1973 in Uruguay and September 1973 in Chile; beginning in March 1976 in Argentina. Only during the 1980s did this repressive context gradually change.

3. Thomas Müntzer in the Context of Liberation Theology: Hugo Echegaray

With the 1976 publication in Lima, Peru, of his essay "Luther and Müntzer: Two Antithetical Conceptions of the Process of Liberation," Hugo Echegaray (1940–79) attested to the interest in Thomas Müntzer in the context of Roman Catholic–influenced Latin American liberation theology. His article appeared in 1976 as a twenty-four-page supplement in the December issue of the journal *Páginas*, which he edited under the auspices of the Center for Studies and Publications. The other articles and illustrations in this issue have a strong liberation theological emphasis. Certain prominent passages make this evident: "Christ does not speak of virtues; it is not a matter of virtue morality, but of justice and compassion" (Echegaray 10), or "Radicality is an elementary requirement to be moral in the eyes of God. Without this radicality one can neither enter into heart of the Gospel nor will the heart of history be transmogrified" (11). This can also be seen in the October 1976 letter of the Brazilian priest and liberation theologian Dom Pedro Maria Casaldáliga, in which he reports on the circumstances in which Pater João Bosco Penido Burnier lost his life at the hands of the Brazilian police when he came to the assistance of two women who had been tortured (51). It was presented by Echegaray as "part of a larger planned work . . . that is currently in preparation" (11) (and which on account of his unexpected early death was never completed).

Echegaray limited himself to literature on Müntzer by Bloch (*Thomas Münzer, teólogo de la revolución*), Norman Cohn (*En pos del milenio* [*The Pursuit of the Millennium*, 1972]), and Hector Vall's thorough 1976 Spanish-language discussion of Walter Elliger's book *Thomas Müntzer, Leben und Werk* (1975). It is therefore clear that Echegaray (like Bahmann before him) was not interested in making a research contribution to the understanding of the dispute between Luther and Müntzer. Instead, the aim of such contributions was to illuminate distinct choices regarding the relationship between Christian faith and political action.

Echegaray offers an empathetic portrayal of Müntzer:

> Insofar as Müntzer leaves aside books and torturous logic, along with his aspiration to guide the consciences of the Saxon princes, he discovered the poor and the illiterate as agents [*agentes*] of the coming kingdom. He had difficulty grasping that the princes are not agents of the Millennium. In Müntzer, a noble vision of the humanity of the poor is apparent; they, who persevered through difficulties, who have suffered, who live neither from avarice nor for luxury

[*lujuria*], but instead care little about the goods of this world, it is they who are preparing a new world. (9–10)

Ultimately, however, the Roman Catholic liberation theologian Echegaray does not find anything in either reformer that takes us genuinely further:

> For both of them, the contemporary world is inevitably lost. Luther therefore tries to ignore it and so retains the cloister perspective of his younger years. Müntzer holds that the world itself deserves to be entirely destroyed. Both await the approaching end of days. Neither Luther—on account of his anthropological pessimism—nor Müntzer—because of his apocalyptic tendencies—perceives with clarity the consistency of secondary causes [*causas segundas*], the responsibility of humans in the field of political action. Müntzer sees only space for a holy war. Luther deprives the political sphere of any moral relevance. In both cases there is a theology of protest that condemns the world, [a theology] in which the transformative role of humans does not attain its true dimension. (20)

Although Echegaray emphasizes Müntzer's empathy for the poor and his rejection of the rich and powerful, he ultimately sees in him no historical model for Christian political action.

4. Writings on Müntzer in the Context of Evangelical Church Academic Institutions in Ibero-America (1980–2006)

While a lecturer on the theological faculty of the Evangelical Church of the Lutheran Confession in Brazil, Martín Norberto Dreher published the 1982 article "The Prophet Thomas Müntzer: Is Thomas Müntzer a Prophet?" In it, he primarily used Carl Hinrichs's treatise *Luther und Müntzer* (1952), Elliger's Müntzer biography, the diverse essay collection on Müntzer edited by Abraham Friesen and Hans-Jürgen Goertz (1978), and as its (practically only) textual basis, the Spanish translation of the "Sermon to the Princes" in Yoder's compilation. For Dreher, Müntzer was "a man who sought to theologically ground revolution," which is why he pursues in his article the questions of "Who was this man?" and "What was his theology?" At the same time, he places him on the side of his "great opponent: Luther," for it is impossible to speak of one without the other: "The tragedy of the one is the tragedy of the other" ("O profeta Thomas Müntzer" 196).

The core of Dreher's article is a detailed examination and interpretation of the "Sermon to the Princes" (202–9). The bottom line: "Müntzer's sermon makes clear that he desires revolution and not the evolution preached by

Luther. The demise of the old [and orthodox] church must not simply lead to the 'word.' At the demise of the old [and orthodox] church, a new social order must arise" (209). After a brief juxtaposition with Luther's doctrine of authority and a nod to the devastating effect of Luther's "Letter to the Princes of Saxony" on Müntzer's life, Dreher states that Müntzer transformed himself into a "prophet of war" on the model of the Old Testament. Turned away from the princes and toward the peasants, Müntzer was "in the last five months of his life an embittered and hate-filled man" (210). He did not rise to his role as leader of the peasant uprising because of his lack of "military and political knowledge." At the end of his article, Dreher concludes that Müntzer

> failed the gospel because for him it was the demand of God and not a possibility for life. It is no accident that the concept of God's grace, revealed in the gospel, did not appear in [Müntzer's] account. . . . Müntzer sought to unite the world with the kingdom of God and in this way fled from reality. As such, he could neither emancipate the peasants from their servitude nor show them a path to emancipation. . . . He announced the Last Judgment but was unable to speak of God's grace. . . . Thomas Müntzer is no prophet in the biblical sense. He is a mystic and an apocalyptic. Nonetheless, in his theology he remains a prophet for us, even though proved catastrophic for both himself and those he sought to help. Müntzer revealed that God's dominion cannot be understood without the inner and outer emancipation of the people. It appears to me [says Dreher] that Müntzer revealed that it is necessary to unify what we today usually keep separate. We tend to hold that either structures must change or humans must be converted. "Müntzer revealed that the human heart is a problem of structures . . . and that structures are a problem of the heart." (Goertz 213–14)

Dreher concludes his work with this quote from Goertz's "Mystic with the Hammer"; he then republished the essay in 1996 with hardly any revisions as the Müntzer chapter titled "Crisis and Renewal of the Church in the Reformation" in the third volume of his church history and again in 2006, incorporating it into his article "Martin Luther and Thomas Müntzer: The Theological Justification of Secular Authority and Political Revolution."

"Decadence of Christianity and Hermeneutics in the Theology of Thomas Müntzer" began as a 1989 examination paper at the Escola Superior de Teologia in São Leopoldo. This thorough piece of research by Luís Henrique Dreher was published the following year in the renowned *Revista eclesástica Brasileira* (L. Dreher). It is one of the few Ibero-American works that builds on a reading of all Müntzer's important writings. Luís Dreher worked with

Müntzer's *Schriften und Briefe*, edited by Gerhard Wehr (1978), and set out "to pursue two basic ideas inherent to Müntzer's theology: [1] his belief that Christianity was in the process of historical decline, and [2] the belief that this [process] can only be understood with a reformulation of the hermeneutic approach" (859).

For his account of Müntzer's "Career and Life," Luís Dreher (859–97) mainly used Manfred Bensing's *Thomas Müntzer Bildbiographie* (1983) and George H. Williams's *Radical Reformation* (Spanish translation, 1983), but also E. Gordon Rupp's *Patterns of Reformation* (1969), Eric W. Gritsch's *Reformer without a Church* (1967), and *The Anabaptists and Thomas Müntzer*, a 1980 essay collection edited by James M. Stayer and Werner O. Packull.

According to Luís Dreher, an idea of "the theological axis around which Müntzer's intellectual world turns" (867) can be best understood within the context of the "theme of the decadence of Christianity" that was so central for Müntzer and is the subject of the article's second section (867–79). In this he observes that Müntzer's

> division [*cisão*] of the concept of faith, according to which "true faith" is valorized and "poetic faith" [*Fe poesía*] devalorized, turns the former into a theoretical instrument that allows Müntzer an *actualization* of the diagnosis of the decline of Christianity. . . . Only this division [*cisão*] makes it possible to call into question the institutional monopolization of Scripture and Church history as tools of self-legitimation of a decadent Christianity, and to help provide them [Scripture and church history] with a universality liberated from false objectivity—false objectivity because it is exclusively produced by the institution itself. (873)

In the third part of the work, titled "Hermeneutics and the New Definition of the Function of Scripture" (879–89), Luís Dreher challenges the (in his opinion exaggerated) pointed contrast in the literature between spirit and letter in Müntzer's theology:

> Müntzer seems to recognize that the much-lauded Scripture is a construct of the time and of the doctors [of theology]; the result of a mystifying interpretational practice, which—since it asserts the objectivity of the Book, it at the same time asserts itself by means of its hegemony, that of its authors and promotors. . . . A proper practice of interpreting Scripture can therefore [for Müntzer] only be legitimate insofar as it arises from suffering; suffering as that unique experience in which God continues to reveal himself just as he did to the Church fathers in biblical times. (884, referring to Müntzer's "Protestation or Proposition," sec. 13).

According to L. Dreher, for Müntzer it was impossible that the Holy Scripture could be read only in light of the tales of the suffering of others (e.g., the patriarchs, the apostles, or Christ) in order to gain salvation. The correct way goes through one's own experience of suffering, as is shown by the example of the common people Mary and Zacharias. In this way Müntzer reaches a reformulation of his hermeneutic approach: "Reading [and understanding] Scripture begins not with the erudition of biblical scholars, but rather amidst the experience of the suffering of common people" (887). Thus, in the last part of his work, where he once again points to the close relationship between the decline/decadence of Christianity and the new hermeneutic approach (889–93), Luís Dreher can say in summary that Müntzer's "epistemological dissent in the assessment of Christianity" is rooted in his sharp separation of "counterfeit" (incapable of suffering) and "genuine" (experiencing suffering) faith (891). Nonetheless, for Müntzer the Bible remains "always irreplaceable, since it records in the testimony of Christ's crucifixion the normative and prototypical form of divine revelation that continues into our historical present" (893). This insightful study by Luís Dreher, building on Müntzer's own theological approach, is perhaps the hitherto most significant Ibero-American contribution to Müntzer scholarship.

In commemoration of the five hundredth anniversary of Luther's birth, a conference was held in September 1983 at the ISEDET where Walter Altmann (lecturer in systematic theology at the Escola Superior de Teología) gave a lecture titled "Confrontation and Liberation: A Latin American Perspective on Martin Luther." Morning seminars with the ISEDET students and faculty on Luther's political and social impact complemented the evening lectures, and his comments about Müntzer came particularly to the fore in a discussion session titled "Resistance and Violence—Selected Texts by Luther about the Peasants." It was evident that students and faculty alike were well acquainted with Müntzer's position toward secular authorities, above all, as Hinrichs described the scene, with reference to his interpretation of Romans 13:

> The situation of both theologians [Luther and Müntzer] is different, and thus their respective interpretations of the text [Rom. 13] are incompatible. One builds on the structure that defends the princes' claim to power, although he recognizes that they abuse this structure. The other reasons from the perspective of the people, in order to highlight such abuses and demand their abolition. . . . Finally we arrive at the conclusion that the evangelical point of view on the problem of violence or non-violence, of the claim to power, of chaos or justice as intellectual approach, is still discussed today in our

churches with the same arguments and the same textual passages with which Luther then justified repressive actions. The variation in such a theology depends on the particular position of any one of us. . . . The question today concerns the bases of polarization from which theology operates: order against chaos, the polarization of the doctrine of national security? Or justice against injustice, the perspective of the biblical option? (Altmann, *Confrontación* 205; see also 203–15).[6]

There was also a criticism raised against Müntzer, based on Carter Lindberg's 1976 article "Theology and Politics: Luther the Radical and Müntzer the Reactionary." As the ISEDET lecturer Mario Yutzis said in his presentation titled "Lindberg Theses,"

> According to Lindberg, Müntzer did not make a clear distinction between the gospel and law. In his utopian view, he thought that it would be possible to govern society with the gospel, i.e., the gospel would itself cause social transformation. Lindberg argues that Müntzer thus makes the gospel into a new law, and as such leads it back into a new legalism. The problem consists in the fact that for Müntzer salvation is an all-conquering end, while for Luther it remains a point of departure. . . . On the other hand, Lindberg argues that while Luther attempts to break out of the model of Christianity insofar as he offers a critique of the clerical structure of power, Müntzer returns to the superseded model of Christianity by means of a perspective that ties it to the peasant class. (Altmann, *Confrontación* 211–12)

Altmann was not, however, fully prepared to accept these claims, agreeing with some but not all of its aspects:

> For example, not the criticism that Müntzer transformed the gospel into a new law. That is Luther's criticism of Müntzer, repeated by Lutherans ever since. I hold that there was a dialectical relationship that we should acknowledge. . . . To be sure, Luther claimed that the legalism present in the Catholic system applied to Müntzer. I do not believe, however, that we should simply repeat this argument today. Müntzer's model is being intensely discussed, and there are opposing views on it. The crucial question is whether his project marks progress, or rather, how much it remains rooted in the medieval model. It seems to be clear that the peasants' movement had tendencies that led back to the time-tested. (214).

It was at the ISEDET (which had the best evangelical library in Ibero-America) that I wrote my theological examination paper "Thomas Müntzer (1489–1525): The Christian Problem of Justice and Order in the Framework of His Conception of History—a Historico-Theological Analysis" (Zorzin). I was able to use not only Müntzer's *Schriften und Briefe*, edited by Günther Franz (1968), but also works by Annemarie Lohmann, Hinrichs, and Elliger, as well as the volume edited by Friesen and Goertz, among other things. Perhaps the most lasting contributions of my first engagement with the tension between justice and order in Müntzer's theology are Spanish translations of his "Open Letter to his brothers in Stolberg," two Allstedt sermon sketches, and his letters to Georg Amandus (March 1524), Johann Zeiss (July 25, 1524), and the people of Mühlhausen (May 17, 1525).

In an article published in 1986 in the *Cuadernos de teología* with the title "Violence and Peace in the Theology of Thomas Müntzer and Dietrich Bonhoeffer," I outlined the interaction of mysticism (existential, or inner dimension) and apocalypticism (historical, or outer dimension) on the basis of relevant passages in Müntzer in order to pursue the question of his statements on peace and violence (Zorzin, "La violencia" esp. 282–87). "There is no peace in the midst of a reality soaked with violence" (286).[7] As pastor in Allstedt, Müntzer came face-to-face with the Reformation's everyday consequences: the local lords' violent persecution of peasants drawn to the Allstedt church services. As I wrote,

> Luther is also aware of this problem, but does not experience it day after day with the same intensity as Müntzer. Their respective proposals [of solutions] for one and the same situation of concrete injustice are therefore different. Luther says that the Christian persecuted because of his evangelical faith should leave the town or city and go elsewhere with the gospel; "leave to the [manorial] lord his city and follow the gospel." (in Luther 323)

"But this proposal remains at the level of theory, for the mechanisms of feudalism do not permit it. Given the problem, it remains at best an individual solution, inapplicable to whole groups persecuted for their faith. Müntzer experiences it first-hand" in July 1524, with the arrival in Allstedt of asylum-seeking refugees from the surrounding Albertine areas. As I wrote at the time,

> The lords of Sangerhausen do not tolerate this massive flight of their subjects, for they thereby lose part of their powers of production! . . . The solution for the situation of an individual cannot be carried over to the group. . . . A communal solution is demanded, and for Müntzer it requires militant violence against a system that is violent in itself. "God's elect must organize themselves in order to defend their faith against the attacks of tyrants." (Zorzin, "La violencia" 286)

I dedicated a 1999 article titled "Apocalyptic Eschatology in the Sixteenth-Century Protestant Reformation: Luther, Müntzer, and the Apocalyptic Anabaptists" to the question of the social relevance and danger of apocalyptic elements in the teachings of Müntzer (and Hans Hut), or rather the social irrelevance and absence of danger of immanent eschatology in Michael Stiefel and Martin Luther (Zorzin, "Escatologia"). Müntzer's apocalyptically informed image of the servants of God sharpening their sickles for the eschatological harvest (which, in the context of the Peasants' Rebellion, he identified with real peasants and miners) was especially virulent because of its connection to his description of the actual "dregs in the pot" (*Grundsuppe*) of social injustice: the lords' and princes' claim of total ownership of all creatures ("Vindication and Refutation"). It is thus clear that Müntzer's prophetic-apocalyptic critique of the existing order was directed at not only the tyrants' godlessness but "also their insatiable economic greed" (37). While in Stiefel or Luther the imminence of the End Times could be felt as acutely as in Müntzer and Hut, the former left the purifying action exclusively to heavenly angels (as was represented in the woodcuts of Albrecht Dürer and Lucas Cranach [31n33]).[8] By contrast, the dissidents (the "radical periphery" of the Reformation), driven by their experience of historical exclusion and impotence as well as an urgency stemming from their insistence on imminent justice, assumed the biblical-apocalyptic model (*esquema*) of their epoch, albeit according to a concrete "script" (*guión*) that made them participants in its execution and realization. This active involvement turned them into recalcitrant and subversive elements. They themselves, after they had cleansed their faith through a process of inner purification, felt themselves to be sent from God (angels), engaged by the Lord to separate the wheat (the pious) from the chaff (godless and tyrants) in the eschatological harvest. (Barthel Betham had represented such an earthly, "wingless" peasant reaper in an illustration in the 1524 Bible printed in Nuremberg by Hans Hergot.) Because they move from merely speculative anticipation of salvation to redemptive action, they are persecuted by the ruling political-religious order, trapped and executed. In contrast to harmless apocalyptics, radical apocalyptics threaten the continued existence of the unjust social system (Zorzin, "Escatologia" 50).

In 1989 the Dutch Reformed Church theologian Enrique Vijver, a lecturer at the ISEDET in the 1980s,[9] composed an article titled "The Actuality of the Controversy between Müntzer and Luther" for the Caracas journal *Presencia ecuménica*. This essay appeared in conjunction with the same issue's Spanish translation of the working group of East Germany's Federation of Evangelical Church's "Orientierungshilfe zum Gedenken des 500. Geburtstages von

Thomas Müntzer im Jahre 1989" ("Declaración"; see also Mau). With reference to the "old controversy" between Müntzer and Luther, Vijver offers "considerations about ethics and meaning (possibilities and limits) of our political action" (6). He therefore keeps his presentation of the positions of both theologians to a minimum. "Fundamental to all of Müntzer's thought and action is his apocalyptic anticipation of the End" (6). Following Heiko A. Oberman, who characterized Müntzer's thought as a theology of the great separation, Vijver summarizes: "War breaks out between the authorities, who did not want to obey God, and the simple people, who turned themselves into Gideon's troop [*tropa*] and will be the instrument of God's reign" (7; see also Oberman 209). In terms of ethical considerations relevant for Latin America, Vijver finds it significant that "Müntzer's thought displays strong utopian strains." Further, Vijver writes, Müntzer holds that

> a small chosen people can transcend the plane of sinfulness, be a sanctified people and accordingly bring out great transformations that are necessary. . . . Müntzer's position does not rest on arguments or concrete facts on which one can construct reasonable debate, but is instead exclusively based on a speculative and hence uncontrollable belief in the coming end of the world, on the foundation of which dispute is impossible. (8)

This position emerges clearly in Münzter, Vijver writes, and "also appears in our time," for example, in the tendency Enrique Dussel represents within Latin American liberation theology (8). In *Ethics and Community* (1986), Dussel claims, according to Vijver,

> that we on the Latin American continent "are experiencing the death throes of an old process and the birth of a new historical order." . . . In this book, Dussel speaks often of saints, heroes, and prophets as founders of a new world. Their struggle stands logically beyond the sinfulness of normal humans, "the struggle of the poor, the subjugated class, is itself the praxis of empire; the struggle against sin; is benign, holy, is virtuous." (Vijver 9; Dussel, *Etica* 99, 188, 193; see also Dussel, *Herrschaft*)

In contrast, with his distinction between two kingdoms, Luther wanted "to emancipate the domain of politics from the eternal tutelage of church and theology; in this sense he is a much more modern thinker than Müntzer. . . . The mixing of religious ideas with politics, which Luther so intensely opposes, regularly occurs in Latin America" (Vijver 9, referring to Schuurman, *Confusio*). Vijver holds that these central ideas of Luther also find parallels in one of the tendencies within Latin American theology, above all in the liberation theologians Juan Carlos Scannone and Clodovis Boff. Both are of the view that "the theological approach [*lo teológico*] must not determine the content of our political programs" (Vijver 9, referring to Boff, Scannone). It is worth noting that the editorial board of this Colombian journal recommends as further reading the books in Spanish translation by Bloch (*Thomas Münzer, teólogo de la revolución*), Engels (*Las guerras*, 1970), Williams (*La reforma radical*), and Yoder (*Textos escogidos*).

In 1988 a conference series dedicated to dialogue between German theology and Latin American (liberation) theology was organized by the Goethe Institute in collaboration with the Ecumenical Research Department (Departamente Ecuménico de Investigación) in San José, Costa Rica. In this setting, Juan Stam, then teaching in the Ecumenical School of Religious Studies at the National University and the Seminario Bíblico Latinoamericano, gave a talk titled "Thomas Müntzer and Latin American Theology," which later appeared in an anthology of these conference proceedings (Stam). With his opening sentence—that Müntzer "was an equally tragic and brilliant figure, a comical mixture of John of Patmos and Don Quixote"—Stam emphasizes Latin American features:

> Like John of Patmos, Müntzer thought apocalyptically, in drastic and dramatic colors. He thundered divine justice against the injustice of his time and dreamt of the Kingdom of God on earth. Like Don Quixote, his head was full of visions, but he lacked the pragmatism and realistic predictability of a Sancho Panza. Nonetheless he was one of the most brilliant leaders of his time and perhaps the one the most daringly consistent in his Christian convictions. (25)

Stam accordingly briefly emphasizes (based on Bloch, Cohn, Williams, Williams and Mergal, and Echegaray) the following: (1) Müntzer as pastoral theologian (workers' pastoral care and the church of the poor) (26–27); (2) Müntzer as contextual theologian (27–29); (3) Müntzer as charismatic theologian (30–32); and (4) Müntzer as revolutionary theologian (32–34). With reference to the "Sermon to the Princes" and other excerpts from Müntzer's writings cited by Bloch, Stam underlines that Müntzer's exegesis

> is time and time again able to illuminate biblical pronouncements with perspectives that remain inaccessible to Luther and Calvin on account of their ideological blockades. . . . What is important in Müntzer's hermeneutics is not his relatively good handling of exegetical method, nor the shortcomings of his interpretation, but rather his implacable resolve to read the Bible from the circumstances of the poor and amidst the struggle of the oppressed. . . . Because of this engagement, Müntzer's hermeneutics were consistently *praxeological*. (29)

In 1999 Jaime Adrián Prieto Valladares, a lecturer at the Universidad Bíblica Latinoamericana, an outgrowth of the Seminario Bíblico Latinoamericano, published the article "Gardens, Dreams, and Enigmas: Müntzer's Apocalyptic Interpretation of Daniel" (Prieto). "Sermon to the Princes," writes Prieto, is in no way "a superficial apocalyptic reading of events in that time of religious, economic, and social uncertainties." In this "key text for understanding the great theological discussions spawned in the historical context of the Reformation and Peasants' War in Central Europe of the 16th century," Müntzer represents the following in parables and symbols:

> a) the creation and humanity as God's vineyard trampled by the corruption of medieval Christianity; b) prophesying, visions, and dreams as means of divine communication for distinguishing the evil from the good; c) the characteristics of true (revealed) divine prophecy, as they arise out of the abyss of the souls of his chosen; d) the significance of Nebuchadnezzar's dream for the Saxon princes. (77)

Prieto remarks that it is difficult to ascertain the extent to which at the time of this sermon Müntzer could have changed "the princes' traditional repressive stance towards the common man, i.e., the miners, cloth weavers, and farmers" (89). Prieto continues,

> Müntzer's sermon addressed to the Saxon princes takes place at a moment of pastoral and theological maturity in his life. While he had earlier passionately embraced the Reformation's messages against clerical abuses and Roman claims to power . . . , in this sermon he sharpens his criticism of Luther's theology of grace and the two kingdoms, the linchpin of princely power. . . . Far from it, in dwelling in this sermon on the Book of Daniel upon a relatively insignificant eschatological interpretation, he arrived at an enormous historic-political dimension. (89)

This overview of the most essential Ibero-American works on Müntzer in the 1980s and 1990s makes two things clear: across Ibero-American interpretations, the basic understanding of Müntzer is informed, unreconstructed, by the works of Bloch, Engels, and (to a certain extent) Williams. Furthermore, there is no reliable Spanish or Brazilian Portuguese (annotated) edition of Thomas Müntzer's writings and (most important) letters that is comparable, for instance, to the exemplary English edition produced by Peter Matheson (Müntzer, *Collected Works*).

5. Fictional Realism: Tomás Munzer in Chiapas

Literary scholars have used the concept of "magical realism" to describe the enchanted transfiguration of reality in Latin America expressed in the

Colombian Gabriel García Márquez's novel *One Hundred Years of Solitude* (1967). In the further development of Latin American novels with historical references and content, such as the Argentine Tomás Eloy Martínez's *Perón Novel* (1985) or *Santa Evita* (1995), this literary mixture of historical facts and nightmarish-seeming plots is in my opinion more fittingly described as "fictional realism."

A quick internet search [in 2010—trans.] for the hispanicized form of Müntzer's name, "Tomás Munzer," brings one to links that indeed can be best subsumed under the general term of Latin American fictional realism. These show that around the time of the recent millennium, Thomas Müntzer became in his own way "indigenous" in Ibero-America. In the Mexican state of Chiapas, in the region of Ocosingo, a small village was named (probably at the beginning of the 1990s) "Primer Agrarista Tomás Munzer."

In the Mexican Revolution, proclaimed four years before the First (European) World War, the concept *agrarista* applied to those leaders who campaigned, like Emiliano Zapata, for the distribution of latifundia lands to the poor Indian population. Ever since, Zapata himself has been considered the first fighter for a general distribution of land in Mexico—the "Primer Agrarista." The giving of the name "Primer Agrarista Tomás Munzer" in a Mexican state like Chiapas, where since the beginning of 1994 the Zapatista Army of National Liberation, supported by the impoverished Mayan population, has fought for a general distribution of land, should at the very least give food for thought. Might this suggest, based on Engels's account of the Peasants' War, an attempt to find a messianic (evangelical) revolutionary role model? It should be kept in mind that Fray Bartolomé de Las Casas (1474–1566) sought a nonviolent path for claiming Indigenous rights against Spanish authorities.

The digital search for "Munzer" in Latin America also reveals a Brigada Tomás Munzer active in Chiapas. By this point, any attempt at interpretation gets lost in the labyrinth of Latin American fictional realism. This Brigada Tomás Munzer is one of the paramilitary groups, sponsored by wealthy large landowners (in the shadows of the Partido Revolucionario Institucional [PRI], the Mexican ruling party), that employed terror to drive Mayan peasants from their primarily communal plots of land and woods.

The Mexican sociologist Jorge Fuentes Morúa, who published an essay with the title "From the Resurrection to the Insurrection" (1994), remarks,

It is in fact extraordinary that peasants from Chiapas decided to baptize one of their organizational entities with the name of Thomas Münzer. As theologian of revolution—according to Bloch—this legendary Christian communist fought to the death on the side of the German peasants who had revolted against the despotism of the landowners. The forceful revolutionary demanded communal ownership of land, water, woods, hunting, and even the singing of the birds. . . . [The city] San Cristóbal [in Chiapas] bears the additional name [of Fray Bartolomé] de Las Casas because collective memory, maintained in the names of villages, streets, and schools, could not forget this worthy representative of a project of a Catholicism that had sought to build on the communal practices of the indigenous population in the newly discovered lands. . . . During the long years of the process of capitalist expansion in the countryside, which coincided with the dispossession of and violence against the original landholders . . . , the ghosts of Múnzer [sic] and Fray Bartolomé have watched with indignant eyes the indescribable violence done to the indigenous population of Chiapas. (30)

Morúa knows that the Münzer district in Chiapas was active on the side of the Mexican ruling party, the PRI. It is for him a clear example of the fact that "in the domain of ideological confrontation the representatives of the powerful classes attempt to monopolize memory for itself; this is a normal procedure for the Mexican ruling party, which, for example, christened the presidential plane with the name 'Emiliano Zapata'" (33n18).

However varied the reception of Thomas Müntzer may be there, a certain homogeneity in the perception of Müntzer is nonetheless unmistakable. And that is an aspect of the *fictional realism* that characterizes this southern American continent and its particular appropriation of Thomas Müntzer. ∎

Alejandro Zorzin is an Uruguayan theologian who trained at the ISEDET in Buenos Aires and the University of Göttingen, where he received his doctorate. Ordained in 1983, he taught church history at the ISEDET from 1990 until 1999, and from 2000 until 2011 he served as pastor of the Friedelsheim Mennonite Community in Germany. From 2012 until 2022, he was a staff member at the Karlstadt-Edition, the complete critical digital edition of the works of Andreas Bodenstein. He has published widely in Spanish and German on the radical Reformation.

Loren Goldman is associate professor of political science at the University of Pennsylvania. He is author of *The Principle of Political Hope* (2023), cotranslator of Ernst Bloch's *Avicenna and the Aristotelian Left* (2019), and is preparing a translation of Bloch's *Thomas Müntzer as Theologian of Revolution* (forthcoming).

ACKNOWLEDGMENTS

Originally published as "Thomas Müntzer, in Lateinamerika," *Thomas-Müntzer-Gesellschaft Veröffentlichungen*, no. 15. Mühlhausen, Germany: Thomas-Müntzer-Gesellschaft, 2010.

1   As Claros writes, "Before a publication was permitted, the censor's office had covered fifty pages with deletions; yet because the press had subscribers and the rights had been paid, the press went to print, and the book saw light of day despite its mutilation" (114).

2   The following discusses only larger works, or those that are points of orientation in the reception history. For a comprehensive study, see Cuadra.

3   See Shaull, *O Cristianismo e a revoluçao social,* "El cambio revolucionario," "El nuevo espíritu revolucionario," and *Hacia una revolución responsable.*

4   See also Lambert Schuurman, a Dutch Reformed Church theologian and lecturer at Instituto Superior Evangélico de Estudios Teológicos (ISEDET, Buenos Aires), who mentions Müntzer twice but accepts skeptical criticisms both times (*El Cristiano* 26, 109).

5   Translator's note: Yoder wrote his introduction and commentary in Spanish; the citations here follow Zorzin's own German translations of Yoder.

6   Translator's note: Altmann's work (*Luther and Liberation*) exists in English translation in both a truncated first (1992) and an expanded second edition (2015); neither contains the transcribed discussions with the audience at the ISEDET, and thus the Spanish edition is followed here, using Zorzin's German translation of the original.

7   A personal experience from my own youth, student days, and time as a vicar under military dictatorships in Uruguay and Argentina (1973-83): During my tenure as a lecturer of church history at the ISEDET (1990-2000), Thomas Müntzer was strongly present, particularly in graduate seminars on the radical Reformation, as well as in primary sources in Spanish translation used as course materials (e.g., Luther's "Letter to the Princes of Saxony," not included in Spanish Luther editions [see Zorzin, course reader], or the anonymous "History of Thomas Müntzer" [Spanish translation in Zorzin, "Perspectivas"]).

8   I follow an unpublished study by Ulrich Bubenheimer (1989) that he kindly shared.

9   Vijver received his doctorate in 1985 at the Free University of Amsterdam with the dissertation "Theologie en bevrijding—een onderzoek naar de relatie tussen eschatology en ethiek in de theologie van G. Gutierrez, J. C. Scannone en R. Alves."

WORKS CITED

Altmann, Walter. *Confrontación y liberación: Una perspectiva Latinoamericana sobre Martín Lutero.* Edited by Juan R. Stumme. Buenos Aires: FOCO-ISEDET, 1987.

Altmann, Walter. *Luther and Liberation: A Latin American Perspective.* Translated by Mary M. Solberg. Minneapolis: Fortress, 1992.

Altmann, Walter. *Luther and Liberation: A Latin American Perspective.* Revised and expanded edition. Translated by Thia Cooper. Minneapolis: Fortress, 2015.

Asendorf, Ulrich. "Die Lehre von den beiden Reichen und die Theologie der Revolution." *Jahrbuch des Martin Luther Bundes* 16 (1969): 34-51.

Bahmann, Manfred. "Un encuentro utópico." *Cuadernos de Teología* 1 (1970): 53-60.

Bainton, Roland H. *Martín Lutero.* Translated by Raquel Lozada and Adam F. Sosa. Buenos Aires: Editorial Sudamericana, 1955.

Bensing, Manfred. *Thomas Müntzer Bildbiographie.* Leipzig: Bibliographisches Institut, 1983.

Betto, Frei. *Batismo de sangue: Os dominicanos e a morte de Carlos Marighella.* Rio de Janeiro: Civilização Brasiliera, 1982.

Betto, Frei. "Debate sobre marxismo—un aporte cristiano revoluccionario." *Revista envio,* no. 91 (1989). https://www.revistaenvio.org/articulo.php/582.

Bloch, Ernst. *Thomas Münzer: Teólogo da revolução.* Translated by Vamireh Chacon and Celeste Aída Galeão. Rio de Janeiro: Biblioteca Tempo Universitário, 1973.

Bloch, Ernst. *Thomas Münzer, teólogo de la revolución.* Translated by Jorge Deike Robles. Madrid: Ciencia Nueva, 1968.

Bloch, Ernst. *Thomas Münzer, théologien de la revolution.* Translated by Maurice de Gandillac. Paris: Juillard, 1964.

Boff, Clodovis. *Teología de lo político: Sus mediaciones.* Salamanca, Spain: Sígueme, 1980.

Bubenheimer, Ulrich. "Symbolik der Revolution: Thomas Müntzer und der Bauernkrieg im Spiegel der Kunst des 16. Jahrhunderts." Typescript. 1989.

Claros, Francisco Rojas. "Una editorial para los nuevos tiempos: Ciencia Nueva (1965–1970)." In *Revista Historia del Presente,* 103–20. Madrid: Departamento de Historia Contemporánea de la UNED, 2005.

Cohn Norman. *En pos del milenio.* Translated by Julio Monteverde Carreño. Barcelona: Barral Rústica, 1972.

Cuadra, Ute Siebert. "Thomas Müntzer y la guerra campesina en Alemania." In *Centro interecelsial de estudios teológicos y sociales, reforma y consuita: América Latina 500 años después,* 29–42. Managua, Nicaragua: Estudios sobre protestantismo e historia, 1989.

"Declaración de las Iglesias Evangélicas de la República Democrática de Alemania sobre los 500 años del nacimiento de Thomas Müntzer." Translated by Akos Puky. *Presencia ecuménica* 14 (1989): 49–50. Originally published as "Orientierungshilfe zum Gedenken des 500. Geburtstages von Thomas Müntzer im Jahre 1989." *Die Zeichen der Zeit* 42, no. 3 (1988): 79–81.

Dreher, Luís Henrique. "Decadência da cristandade e hermenêutica na teologia de Thomas Müntzer." *Revista eclesiástica Brasileira* 50, no. 200 (1990): 858–95.

Dreher, Martín N. "A crise e a renovação de igreja no período da reforma." In vol. 3 of *Coleção historia da igreha,* 79–93. São Leopoldo, Brazil: Sinodal Editora, 1996.

Dreher, Martín N. "Martinho Lutero (1483–1546) e Tomás Müntzer (1489–1525): A justificação teológica da autoridade secular e da revoluçao política." *Veritas* 51, no. 3 (2006): 145–68.

Dreher, Martín N. "O profeta Thomas Müntzer: Thomas Müntzer, um profeta?" *Estudios teológicos* 22, no. 3 (1982): 195–214.

Dussel, Enrique. *Etica comunitaria: Liberta o pobre!* Buenos Aires: Editiones Paulinas, 1986.

Dussel, Enrique. *Herrschaft und Befreiung: Ansatz, Stationen und Themen einer lateinamerikanischen Theologie der Befreiung.* Freiburg im Breisgau, Germany: Edition Exodus, 1985.

Echegaray, Hugo. "Lutero y Munzer: Dos concepciones antitéticas del proceso de liberación." *Páginas* 7 (1976): 1–24.

Elliger, Walter. *Thomas Müntzer, Leben und Werk.* Göttingen, Germany: Vandenhoek and Ruprecht, 1975.

Engels, Federico. *Las guerras campesinas en Alemania*. Translated by Pedro Peralta. La Plata, Argentina: Editorial Calomino, 1946.

Engels, Federico. *Las guerras campesinas en Alemania*. Buenos Aires: Editorial Andes, 1970.

Friesen, Abraham, and Hans-Jürgen Goertz, eds. *Thomas Müntzer*. Darmstadt, Germany: Wissenschaftliche Buchgesellschaft, 1978.

Gritch, Eric W. *Reformer without a Church: Thomas Müntzer*. Philadelphia: Fortress, 1967.

Hinrichs, Carl. *Luther und Müntzer: Ihre Auseinandersetzung über Obrigkeit und Widerstandsrecht*. Berlin: De Gruyter, 1952.

Lindberg, Carter. "Theology and Politics: Luther the Radical and Müntzer the Reactionary." *Encounter* 37, no. 4 (1976): 356–71.

Lohmann, Annemarie. *Zur geistigen Entwicklung Thomas Müntzers*. Leipzig: Teubner, 1931.

Luther, Martin. "Ermahnung zum Frieden auf die zwölf Artikel der Bauerschaft in Schwaben. 1525." In vol. 18 of *D. Martin Luthers Werke: Kritische Gesamtausgabe*, 279–334. Weimar: Hermann Böhlau, 1908.

Mau, Rudolf. "Rollentausch bei der Müntzerrezeption? Zum Müntzerverständnis im Gedenkjahr 1989." *Berliner Theologische Zeitschrift* 7, no. 1 (1990): 66–77.

Morua, Jorge Fuentes. "De la resurrección a la insurrección." *Iglesias* 10, no. 127 (1994): 25–33.

Müntzer, Thomas. *The Collected Works*. Translated and edited by Peter Matheson. Edinburgh: T & T Clark, 1988.

Müntzer, Thomas. *Schriften und Briefe*. Edited by Gerhard Wehr. Gütersloh, Germany: Gütersloher Verlagshaus Mohn, 1978.

Müntzer, Thomas. *Thomas Müntzer: Schriften und Briefe, Kritische Gesamtausgabe*. Edited by Günther Franz. Gütersloh, Germany: Gütersloher Verlagshaus Mohn, 1968.

Oberman, Heiko A. "Thomas Müntzer: Van Verontrusting tot Verzet," *Kerk en Theologie* 24 (1973): 205–14.

Prieto Valladares, Jaime Adrián. "Jardines, sueños y enigmas (interpretación apocalíptica de Daniel según Thomas Müntzer)." *Vida y pensamiento* 19, no. 2 (1999): 76–92.

Rupp, E. Gordon. *Patterns of Reformation*. Philadelphia: Fortress, 1969.

Scannone, Juan Carlos. "Das Theorie-Praxis Verhältnis in der Theologie der Befreiung." In *Befreiende Theologie*, edited by Karl Rahner, 77–96. Stuttgart: W. Kohlhammer, 1977.

Schuurman, Lambert. *Confusio regnorum: Studie zu einem Thema aus Luthers Ethik*. The Hague: van Keulen Periodieken, 1965.

Schuurman, Lambert. *El Cristiano, la iglesia y la revolución*. Buenos Aires: Junta de Publicaciones de las Iglesias Reformades, 1970.

Shaull, Richard. "El cambio revolucionario en un perspectiva teológica." *Cristianismo y sociedad* 4, no. 12 (1966): 49–69. English: "Revolutionary Change in Theological Perspective," in John Bennett, ed., *Christian Social Ethics in a Changing World: An Ecumenical Theological Inquiry*, 23–43. New York: Association Press, 1966.

Shaull, Richard. "El nuevo espíritu revolucionario de América latina." *Cristianismo y sociedad* 1, no. 3 (1963–64): 30–43.

Shaull, Richard, ed. *Hacia una revolución responsible: Ensayos sobre socio-ética Cristiana*. Buenos Aires: Aurora, 1970.

Shaull, Richard. *O Cristianismo e a revoluçao social*. São Paolo: UCEB, 1953.

Stam, Juan. "Tomas Müntzer y la teología Latinoamericana." In *Teología Alemana y teología Latinoamericana de la liberación: Un esfuerzo de diálogo*, edited by Franz Hinkelammert et al., 25–35. San José de Costa Rica: Departamento Ecuménico de Investigación, 1990.

Stayer, James M., and Werner O. Packull. *The Anabaptists and Thomas Müntzer*. Dubuque, IA: Kendall/Hunt, 1980.

Vall, Hector. "Review of Walter Elliger, *Thomas Müntzer: Vida y obra*." *Actualidad bibliografica de filosofía y teología* 13 (1976): 103–13.

Vijver, Enrique. "La actualidad de la controversia entre T. Müntzer y M. Lutero." *Presencia ecuménica* 14 (1989): 6–10.

Williams, George H. *La reforma radical*. Translated by Antonio Alatorre. Mexico City: Fondo Cultura Económica, 1983.

Williams, George H., and Angel M. Mergal, eds. *Spiritual and Anabaptist Writers*. Louisville, KY: Westminster John Knox, 1957.

Yoder, John Howard, ed. *Texts escogidos de la reforma radical*. Translated by Nélida Meilaharzu de Machain and Ernesto Suárez Vilela. Buenos Aires: Aurora, 1976.

Zorzin, Alejandro. Course reader for "Reforma radical." Buenos Aires: ISEDET, first semester, 2000.

Zorzin, Alejandro. "Escatología apocalíptica en la reforma protestante del siglo XVI: Martín Lutero, Tomás Müntzer y los anabaptistas apocalípticos." In *Escatología y espiritualidad. Expectativas de fin de milenio*, edited by Mario Cayota, Alejandro Zorzin, and Claudio Bedriñán, 21–68. Montevideo: Centro Emmanuel, 1999.

Zorzin, Alejandro. "La violencia y la paz an las teologías de Thomas Müntzer y Dietrich Bonhoeffer." *Cuadernos de teología* 7, no. 4 (1986): 281–301.

Zorzin, Alejandro. "Perspectivas protestantes en la historia." In *Ensayos y documentos: Martín Lutero—Felipe Melanchthon—Dietrich Bonhoeffer*, 124–44. Buenos Aires: self published, 1997.

Zorzin, Alejandro. "Thomas Müntzer (1489–1525): La problemática Cristiana de la justicia y del orden en el marco de su cosmovision histórica—Un análisis histórico y teológico." Buenos Aires. Typescript. 1980.

O. L. Silverman

"We Are Free and We Wish to Be Free"
Political Thought and the Peasants' War

ABSTRACT This essay explores the symptomatic absence of the German Peasants' War (1525)—the largest popular uprising in Europe before the French Revolution—from classical political thought. It begins with Leo Strauss's and Sheldon Wolin's appraisals of what united the body of literature, namely, that the role of the political theorist is to articulate and advocate visions of order. The abundant archive of peasant demands, sermons, ordinances, territorial constitutions, and prophecies were inscrutable to the order-oriented assumptions of traditional political philosophy. First, because the theory produced in the struggle was not separate from insurgent action. The uprising was led, articulated, and theorized by those who were dismissed as fanatics rather than engaged by authorities and by political thinkers like Sir Thomas More. The essential unit of organization and voice of the Peasants' War was collective—no singular author appears to reflect on the conjuncture from a detached vantage. The political aims of this period were at once theological, existential, and economic. These aims were expressed through a "political theology of ingression" whose key gesture was to bridge separations. Peasants sought to literalize metaphor and to discern the literal as already allegorical: the material condition of serfdom was simultaneously a form of spiritual bondage; biblical images of divine common life could be actualized by sharing life, land, and goods on earth.

KEYWORDS German Peasants' War, classical political thought, fanaticism, political theology, Thomas Müntzer, *omnia sunt communia*

It was the largest popular uprising in Europe until the French Revolution, and yet, we can't quite recall it. The German Peasants' War (1524–25) was a monumental rebellion against serfdom; against the consolidating regime of private property; against the predatory extraction of rents, taxes, and tithes; and against the authority of feudal princes, lords, and clergy. Imperial palaces, castles, princely fortresses, and the monasteries of ecclesiastical landlords were emptied, redistributed, and set aflame (Blickle 18). Directed by popular peasant assemblies, the uprising was led by three hundred thousand peasants, miners, weavers, artisans, serfs, vagrants, and commoners across five major

HISTORY of the PRESENT ▪ A Journal of Critical History ▪ 15:1 ▪ April 2025
DOI: 10.1215/21599785-11561531 © 2025 Duke University Press

regions in German-speaking lands of the Holy Roman Empire (Baylor, *German Reformation* 1, 24). This number neglects the uncounted women who likely flanked and fed peasant armies, or those, after the men had left to fight, who tilled fields and descended into silver mines (Roper, "Emotions" 63), and the women who took up pitchforks and rang storm bells themselves (Drummond 141; Roper, "Emotions" 63; Roper, "'Common Man'" 14). Even the largest national armies of the period, like that of France, only numbered in the tens of thousands (Baylor, *German Reformation* 1). By any estimate, the peasant rebellion was a supernova.

The uprising was also a wellspring of political writing, taking hold in a moment of expanding literacy in the lower classes (Edwards 38–40): in two years, more than one hundred articles, ordinances, and constitutions were published and widely circulated, giving voice to collective demands. Insurgent armies and assemblies worked through horizontal modes of direct decision-making. Positions of military and religious authority were chosen by direct election and subject to popular recall (Baylor, *German Reformation* 22–26; Blickle 91, 122). The fulmination of popular participation in the revolt certainly evinced forms of mass political thought. Yet, in the pages of thinkers like Hobbes, Locke, and Montesquieu, whose meditations spanned political history from antiquity onward, the German Peasants' War is a nonevent. It was not until the nineteenth century that the Peasants' War substantially entered the field of political thought with the publication of Friedrich Engels's *Peasant War in Germany* (1850). From Engels through today, with a few notable exceptions, most significantly Ernst Bloch, the Peasants' War remains largely overlooked as a locus for political theorization. What, then, does the peculiar omission of the German Peasants' War in the history of political thought express?

The upswell of scholarly attention to the Haitian revolution (James; Trouillot; Buck-Morss; Fischer; Scott; Joseph; Nesbitt; Dubilet) offers damning testimony that the most defining political events of modernity have been silenced or disavowed by canonized political thought. Predictably, the most detonating critiques have come from outside provincial Europe. The German Peasants' War didn't occur on another continent, however, but quite loudly and conspicuously in the middle of Early Modern Europe. Yet it, too, remains, to borrow a phrase from Michel-Rolph Trouillot, a largely "silenced" past. The question then is not, Why was the German Peasants' War excluded from political thought? but rather, What is symptomatic about its absence? This question draws inspiration from recent scholarly efforts to reorient theory from portrait to panorama; to shift from the above-the-neck bust of the political theorist to view an entire body in a conflictual social field. In turn, it follows work that attends to how political actors in mass movements themselves have produced ingenious theories, frames, and imaginaries (Pineda 18). To this end, Massimiliano Tomba writes that we must abandon "the privileged point of view of both great theorists and leaders, but not to substitute them with other leaders or figures marginalized by the dominant historiography. . . . [This] is about considering the practice of insurgents as theory in action that goes to constitute the collective ink with which the political documents of an insurgency are written" (2). The task does not simply rest on including the excluded. Tomba provokes us to resist the impulse to rewrite heroic narratives with new, previously marginalized leaders. The challenge is that real democracy cannot be thought through the schemas of leaders or authors, and so attention to insurgent moments itself remakes the very grammar and methods of political thought.

To ask after the symptomatic absence of the Peasants' War in the canon, this essay begins with Leo Strauss's and Sheldon Wolin's appraisals of what united the body of literature, namely, that the role of the political theorist is to articulate and advocate visions of order. In the second half of the essay, I turn to the abundant archive of documents from the Peasants' War to examine the modes of writing and organization of the insurgent German peasants. These texts reveal that the fundamental forms of peasant textuality and organization render them inscrutable to the order-oriented assumptions of traditional political philosophy.

This essay traces the key dimensions of the opposition that the Peasants' War archive poses to the canon of political thought. In the first two sections, I explore the role of the emergence of the modern figure of the fanatic during the Peasants' War and the view of fanaticism from the vantage of political theory. In the third section, I highlight the active nature of texts during this period and the distinctively collective character of theoretical production. In contrast to the political-philosophical treatise with its "preferred genres of reflection" (Vázquez-Arroyo 150), for the insurgents, writing and textuality were change-oriented instruments of political action. Against the solitary profile of the individual theorist, I suggest that the basic unit of organization and voice in the Peasants' War was a collective one. In the second half of the essay, I introduce the opposition of peasant theory to canonical political thought through an exploration of the political theology of the peasants. The political dimensions of the German Peasants' War were indissociable from its economic, theological, and social aspects. The abolition of the separation of these realms, like divine and civil authority, was also an active ambition of the peasants. This aim took the form of what I call the "political theology of ingression," a form whose internal logic is constitutively unreadable to architectonic political theories that fortify enduring visions of order.

The key gesture of the political theology of ingression was to bridge separations to literalize metaphor and to apprehend the literal as itself already allegorical: the material condition of serfdom was simultaneously a form of spiritual serfdom; biblical images of common life could be actualized by sharing land and goods on earth. The political "theology of ingression" describes the endeavor to join the word and the deed, the head and the heart, necessity and freedom, and heaven and earth. This political theology subverted the separations that subtended the social order. The lords and clergy understood the peasants as both living forms of property (serfs) *and* the embodiment of disorder (insurgents). To bring the German Peasants' War and its antagonisms into a more direct encounter with the history of political thought is to shift from a vantage of order to the visions of those for whom the dominant order *was* a crisis.

Order and/as Political Theory

Despite their many disagreements, two of the leading political theorists contending with the behavioralist turn of the mid-century, Sheldon Wolin and Leo Strauss, both argued that what distinguished the role of the political theorist was the ability to transform perception into an imaginative view of the social whole. This is to say: the political theorist produces a vision of order. In his 1957 essay "What Is Political Philosophy?" Leo Strauss proposes that "the guiding theme of political thought" was "the regime" or "the order, the form, which gives society its character" (363). Order encompasses the form of life, style, morality, government, and form of state (363). For Strauss, *politeia* is the principle that organizes order, and thus political philosophy aims to ascertain "both the nature of political things and the right or the good, political order" (367).

Although Wolin disagreed with Strauss's moralism, which he thought masqueraded as a politics (i.e., the suggestion that there was one good political order), the holism of political thought was a point of concord between the two. Wolin defines the role of the political theorist as one shared with philosophers, namely, "the quest for order" or "the basic quest for systematic knowledge" that offers a view of public matters that "concern the whole community" (*Politics and Vision* 4). Order, Wolin suggests, is defined by an irrepressible "architectonic impulse" to bring order to cosmological chaos (20). "The essential element present in political philosophy," he writes, is "the ideal of an order subject to human control and one that could be transfigured through a combination of thought and action" (20). In Wolin's view, the canon of European political thought emerges with the appearance of the political theorist in a specialized role: Machiavelli, Hobbes, Locke, Rousseau, and Montesquieu responded to the major social crises they witnessed (9). Thus the traditional task of the political philosopher is one of "encompasser of disorder" (9). To encompass means to encircle, to draw up a boundary that separates, with the first step to "fashion a political cosmos out of political chaos" (9). The goals of political theory, Wolin suggests, have been twofold: first, the prognostication of disaster, and second, "attaining ends which, for one reason or another, one deemed good or desirable" (14).

The "architectonic impulse" of political philosophy in Wolin's thought was analytically distinct from the politics of democracy:

> Institutionalization marks the attenuation of democracy: leaders begin to appear; hierarchies develop; experts of one kind or another cluster around the centers of decision; *order*, procedure, and precedent displace a more spontaneous politics: in retrospect the latter appears as disorganized, inefficient. *Democracy thus seems destined to be a moment rather than a form. Throughout the history of political thought virtually all writers emphasize the unstable and temporary character of democracy. Why is it that democracy is reduced, even devitalized by form?* Why is its presence occasional and fugitive? (Wolin, *Fugitive Democracy* 108; my emphasis)

For Wolin, democracy is a formless, fugitive moment of spontaneous politics, a breach that becomes an object for the writers who theorize it. Democracy is "a mode of being which is conditioned by bitter experience" (111). It is a paradox that democracy is "a political moment, perhaps the political moment, when the political is remembered and recreated" (111), and yet democracy is distinct from the activity called political thought. The tension between political theory and democracy evokes an even more fundamental conflict: between thought and action. The analytical gap between the theorist and the experience of democracy, for Wolin, a deeply historically sensitive thinker, was likely more of a descriptive than normative claim. The canonized texts of political thought so often understood democracy as a crisis of order and a problem of thought. But the extant texts from the German Peasants' War blur these distinctions; they betray the political visions of those who *were* the disaster and not its prognostication.

Amid political theory's general field of silence, the Peasants' War *can* be found in the writings of one canonical thinker: Sir Thomas More. Without comparing publication dates, one might intuitively assume that More's *Utopia* was conversant with the events in Germany. After all, the most radical demand of the Peasants' War, "*omnia sunt communia*," was an organizing principle of More's ludic holiday work. The "thing that Plato *imagines in* his republic . . . the Utopians *actually practice* in theirs," More wrote, namely, that "all things are held in common (*omnia sunt communia*)" (*Utopia* 98; my emphasis). But *Utopia* (1516) was written a decade before the Peasants' War, and, over the course of that decade, More obsessively polemicized against the heretical attempts in Germany and England to actualize the arrangement found in the Acts of the Apostles and his *Utopia*. He located the German peasants within a rich, international tradition of heresy that led to earthly revolt:

> In Africa the Donatists; in Greece the Arians; in Bohemia the Hussites; in England the Wycliffists; and now in Almaine [Germany] the Lutherans. . . . And thus is it sure that by their false doctrine they must, if they be believed, bring the people into the secret contempt, and spiritual disobedience, and *inward hatred of the law; whereof must after follow the outward breach, and thereupon outward punishment and peril of rebellion*—whereby the princes should be driven to sore effusion of their subjects' blood, as hath already mishappened in Almaine and, of old time, in England. (More, *Essential Works* 810–11; my emphasis)

More understood that heresy was forged by inner experience that turned into an "outward breach," which flowered in rebellion. "The past centuries," More winced, "have not seen anything more monstrous than the [German] Anabaptists" (352). What distinguished the expressions of *"omnia sunt communia"* in his *Utopia* from those of the Peasants' War was their methods. *Utopia* was a propertyless nowhere-commonwealth concocted in an individual imagination, an interior "mental event" (Manuel and Manuel 26) separated from "outward expression." During the Peasants' War, experience, experimentation, visions, and dreams guided armies in violent rebellion for a common life. If *Utopia* was a synthetic fantasy of a well-ordered commonwealth, modeled on Plato's *Republic*, then the Peasants' War was the real and explosive appearance of inward consciousness and outward rebellion of the lower classes. Reading More, the Peasants' War is neither an omission nor a conspicuous silence, but rather a symptomatic fixation with an object of terror and heresy.

Fanaticism against Order

The figure of the fanatic, as the embodiment of disorder, has had a privileged place in the history of political thought as its antonymic outside or other. Another answer to Strauss's question, "What Is Political Philosophy?" was, in brief: *not* fanaticism. Classical political philosophy, whose spirit is "serenity and sublime sobriety," Strauss intones, "is free from all fanaticism because it knows that evil cannot be eradicated and therefore that one's expectations from politics must be moderate" (356–57). The enterprise of political philosophy is thus defined against fanaticism, and, in turn, fanaticism is identified as the belief that evil can be expunged. This was a rather conspicuous importation of the notion of original sin to politics: to understand politics, for Strauss, was to accept the premise of the fallenness of man. The argument for the acceptance of evil doubles as an argument against radical social ends, like the elimination of private property, and thus, Strauss alleges, political philosophy is constitutionally moderate. If the fanatic is political thought's antonymic shadow, then the term's modern historical appearance, forged in the crucible of the German Peasants' War, opens a view of the fundamental challenges that the event poses to traditional political philosophy.

Fanaticism derives from the Latin *fanum* or temple. The term appears as early as the first century in Cicero's descriptions of "superstitious" or "absurd" philosophers (*De Divinatione* 505). As scholars of fanaticism Dominique Colas, Alberto Toscano, and Ross Lerner have elucidated, the modern sense of the word *fanaticism* as a term of abuse appeared during the Reformation to describe the protagonists of the German Peasants' War (Colas; Toscano; Lerner). The German word for fanatic, *Schwärmer*, related to English "swarmers" and sometimes translated as "enthusiasts," was used by theologians and civil authorities to describe the sudden appearance of roving assemblies of peasants that moved together with the at once chaotic and collected energies of a swarm. The account of George Metzler, an innkeeper from Ballenberg, recorded shortly after the 1525 uprising is illustrative: "The peasants formed mobs and rallied from all the surrounding places swarmed to the band like bees to the hive and accepted the Twelve Articles" (Scott and Scribner 243). Several years later, Martin Luther and his closest collaborator, Philip Melanchthon, would denounce the Anabaptists as fanatics. In the Smalcald Articles, a summary of Lutheran doctrine written more than a decade after the Peasants' War, Luther warns against "the fanatics [*Schwärmer*], the "spirits," who boast that they have the Spirit apart from and before contact with the Word. . . . [Thomas] Müntzer did this, and there are still many doing this today who set themselves up as shrewd judges between the spirit and the letter without knowing what they say or teach" (*Ninety-Five Theses* 188). Here Luther describes the peasants' political theology of the Holy Spirit, exemplified in Thomas Müntzer's sermons. Müntzer, a key theologian of the insurgent German peasants, rejected the Lutheran doctrines of *sola scriptura*, the view that faith was conferred through the Bible alone, and *fides ex auditu*, the notion that faith was imparted through hearing the scripture read. Across the German lands of the Holy Roman Empire, the Catholic Church conducted the liturgy in Latin, a fortress language unknown to its congregations. The theologians of the Peasants' War biblically justified the abandonment of the hierarchical structures of the late Middle Ages in favor of a theology of the Holy Spirit that authorized the poor to communicate directly with God, relieving them of their dependence on the written Latin word and its sentinels. Indeed, in their practical theological and political organizations, they became their own judges on a literal register, electing pastors and military leaders who were subject to popular recall. More elementally, Luther's description of the *Schwärmer* illustrates the characteristic features of fanaticism. The fanatics blended belief and political vision with radical action. "Setting themselves up as shrewd judges between the spirit and the letter," the fanatics think *and* act. They self-authorize.

The radical political theological view that evil *could* be eliminated, what Strauss would have termed the peasants' "fanaticism," manifested as radical demands: the abolition of serfdom; common access to fishing waters, meadows, and forests; the respect of the political autonomy and authority of town assemblies; and even a call for common property (Scott and Scribner 72, 81, 252–57, 437). In this sense, the Swabian League, Luther, and civil authorities used the term *fanaticism* in a remarkably similar register to Strauss's construction of fanaticism, the embodied view that evil could be extinguished, against political theory whose vision was "constitutionally moderate." Despite, or perhaps because of their new political legibility in the form of written demands, the chosen title for the insurgent peasants, *Schwärmer*, conjured the inhuman association of an acephalic swarm of insects, a leaderless mob consumed by a novel form of madness. As an example of the eruption of fanaticism, the Peasants' War, then, is not a simple omission of classical political thought. Rather, it reveals political thought's phobic obsession with a form of radical praxis that is pathologized in the margins of texts and noncanonical writings rather than engaged with.

Collective Voice and Authorial Action

The image of the swarm evokes a distinct shape that, only on a disquieting, second glance, appears as the immense collection of individual bodies. In this sense, the fearful descriptions of the peasants as *Schwärmer* reveal another dimension of the Peasants' War that distinguished it from canonical political thought. The basic unit of organization and voice was a collective one: the place of thought occurred laterally, in the commune and the band (*Bund*). The rebellion took shape in the already-existing infrastructure of village communes and assemblies of male landowners (Scott and Scribner

14). To "make a ring" or "hold a commune" were the expressions villagers used to call for a circle of mutually dependent equals who gathered around the village oak tree to deliberate (14). In 1524 revolt broke out when communes halted their agricultural labor to assemble for protest marches in which communes formed regional bands (Baylor, *German Reformation* 23). The membership of bands extended beyond that of the exclusive equality of the village commune, as renters and small landowners gained an equal part in decision-making (24). Bands were military, religious, and political unions: the band was established by an oath, to each other and to God, and they operated by democratic assembly, learned in the commune (24). During the rebellion, some peasant bands began to identify as a *Landschaft*, a term that signified the inhabitants of a region and, in some regions, a representative assembly of different classes.[1] *Landschaft* named a collectivity that extended far beyond the legally constituted boundaries of the village commune, and was often invoked in peasant texts as "men and women, rich and poor" (Scott and Scribner 17).

It was in collective assemblies that bands envisioned and theorized their conditions and common goals. Collective theorization took the form of lists of peasant demands, widely disseminated articles, field ordinances, constitutions, and sermons, forms that themselves *enacted* their demands in demonstrations of popular power and consciousness. The most broadly circulated program, "The Twelve Articles," was composed in Memmingen in 1525 by peasant bands from three regions who formed a "peasant parliament" (Baylor, *German Reformation* 76). Sebastian Lotzer, a fur dealer and lay preacher, condensed three hundred articles produced by the Baltringen peasants into twelve to be presented to the Swabian League, and Christoph Schappeler, another partisan preacher, provided biblical citations for the articles (Scott and Scribner 243, 252). Thomas Müntzer, Sebastian Lotzer, and Christoph Schappeler were hailed as singular authors and leaders by the authorities of the time and by archivists and historians after them. However, these men saw their role as intermediaries for collective voices rather than as leaders. Preachers often acted as secretaries for regional peasant bands and assemblies, transcribing peasant demands, providing scriptural support, and sustaining the morale of peasant armies (Baylor, *German Peasants War* 23). Lists of demands recorded in mass assemblies; public, polemical letters; and fiery, chiliastic sermons calling for an end to serfdom expressed their own distinct theoretical forms.

If the genre of the political philosophical treatise was primarily reflective, the theoretical forms of the peasants were at once philosophical and practical.

The articles, constitutions, field ordinances, grievances, and sermons marked the appearance of a written record of the peasants' perspective (who comprised 80 percent of the population of Germany). Like the manifesto, these texts are forms of "change-writing" (Ebert 554). The peasant documents act, and they reflect; they are at once forms of "transformative textuality" and the "textuality of transformation" (554).

Like the village assembly, the church congregation was also a venue for change-writing as sermons and the new vernacular German liturgy transformed the everyday experience of Mass for the German people into a site of political consciousness. Just as the theologian took a supportive role in peasant bands, in the congregation, the priest was no longer a master mediator between God and the congregation. He was a guide who shared what he had read in the scripture and what he had discovered from his own experience of faith (Müntzer 19). In this spirit, Thomas Müntzer produced a new liturgy in vernacular German with music and a book of common prayer. The score of Müntzer's *German Church Service Book* (1523) was taken from existing Gregorian melodies, which, Andy Drummond speculates, were chosen because their tones would be familiar to the ears of the congregation (110). This marked a monumental shift in perspective and mood; a single Latin voice no longer fell from the podium to the ears below, and in churches all over Germany, the service was suddenly, collectively sung. "For once," Drummond writes, "the parishioners would actually be participating and understanding the words" (110). This transformation was accompanied by a literal revolution of the preacher, in that the preacher, who had previously faced the altar, now rotated 180 degrees to face the congregation (113). One can imagine the shock in orientation to hear song and scripture resounding panoramically from the mouths of the peasants, weavers, and miners on the floors of congregations. Like the scenes of assembly and battle, the shift in attention from an elevated man to oneself as part of a collective-in-song on the floor in the congregation marked the appearance of a kind of "choral politics" of lateral resonance and concerted action (Hanley). New vernacular translations of the Bible and the German church service supplied peasants with biblical justifications for their revolt against church authority. But the vernacular translations were also a form of action unto themselves, catalyzing the active participation of the lower classes in pursuit of their own salvation. From a sociological vantage, collective voice and the particularly transformative character of textuality and authorial action were two essential forms that characterized the theory-in-action of the Peasants' War. This register, however, is still a level removed from how the peasants articulated their own experience of revolutionary transformation.

The Political Theology of Ingression

The distinctive modes of the peasants, like collective voice, were unintelligible to the authorities of their time and classical political thought after 1525. To the princes of Germany, they appeared as alien forms (or, more precisely, as alien swarms). In one year, peasants produced a voluminous archive of texts from the perspectives inside the swarm. South of Germany in the same period, Nicolò Machiavelli was composing the theory credited with cleaving political authority from theology and morality (Skinner 381). For the German peasants, who were products of the order of the Middle Ages, the theological, social, and economic were not thought to be separate topoi or distinct realms. Earthly law was grounded in divine right, the clergy were also rapacious landlords, and God could be appealed to against the authority of the nobility. Further, the abolition of the consolidating division between civil and divine authority was also a concerted aim of the peasants.

The union of the political, economic, and theological character of the peasants' demands is best understood through their self-justifications, which were articulated in a theology of the Holy Spirit, or what I call a "political theology of ingression." I lift the term *ingression* from Herbert Marcuse's *Essay on Liberation* (1969) where he describes a revolutionary conjuncture marked by a shift in consciousness and "sensitivity" adequate to the overcoming of capitalist social relations.[2] This shift, Marcuse writes, is attended by "the ingression of freedom into the realm of necessity" (20), "the ingression of the aesthetic and the political" (29), and "the ingression of the future into the present" (61). The goals of the struggle "for qualitatively different ways of life" appear in and through the process of rebellion itself (20). "In short," he muses, "the economic, political, and cultural features of a classless society must have become the basic needs of those who fight for it" (61). What 1525 shares with Marcuse's view of 1968 is that a moment of struggle produced the qualitatively different sensibility required for the reproduction of collective life. The peasants' insurrectionary political theology was marked by the ingression of the deed into the word, the head into the heart, the spirit into the body, and heaven into earth.

The political theology of ingression understood the separation of the theological, economic, and political as expressions of the decay of real faith. This belief generalized the crisis of authority with images of an inverted world: the avaricious practices of lords and monasteries—levying a death tax on serfs, barring access to common lands, extracting excessively high rents, and restricting marriages (Blickle 57)—attested to the distance of the upper classes from God. From the mid-fifteenth century (ca. 1450) through approximately 1630, the economy and population of German lands experienced a period of marked expansion (Baylor, *The German Reformation* 4). These years saw a "price revolution" in which ballooning inflation resulted in increasingly unfavorable economic conditions for peasants and commoners (4). Landlords took advantage of this shift by ruthlessly raising rents and fees, reimposing serfdom, and reclaiming exclusive usufruct rights for common lands that peasants relied on for subsistence activities (4). From the peasants' vantage, the hypocrisies of the social order were based on a doctrine of separation, and the political theology of ingression emerged to articulate and reunite what had been held apart for the purposes of social control. Jacob Taubes suggests that Thomas Müntzer's political theology sublated the division between Kierkegaard and Marx—between the inner life of the individual, the "religious reality of the passion of spiritual action," and the social life of the masses (118). Like Taubes, numerous studies of the revolutionary character of peasant political theology have gathered around Müntzer (Bloch; Goertz *Thomas Müntzer: Apocalyptic, Mystic and Revolutionary*; Ozment; Drummond). The following section reads the wider archive across peasant texts to demonstrate that Müntzer's voice was part of a chorus of the popular expression of the political theology of ingression.

The most comprehensive justification for the Peasants' War was anonymously published at the peak of the uprising in May 1525, and it was circulated in Nuremberg and later attributed to Schappeler. "To the Assembly of the Common Peasantry" argued for the right of insurrection, the necessity of "a communal government" (Baylor, *The German Reformation* 112), and the ungodliness of unjust authority, hereditary and monarchal rule, and serfdom. The social order depended on principles far afield of the common good and the divine injunction to "love one another" (Romans 13:8). Of all texts written during the rebellion, chapter 7 of the tract, "Whether a community may depose its authorities or not?," advanced the clearest statement of the political theology of ingression:

> May God pity us that such fleshly authority should rule over Christian people. And unceasingly they may talk about two kinds of commandments, namely the divine, which concerns the salvation of the soul, and the political, which concerns the common good. *Oh God, these commandments cannot be separated from each other. For the political commandments are also divine*: truly to further the common good is nothing except to maintain brotherly love, which is of the highest merit for blessedness. (Baylor, *German Reformation* 121; my emphasis)

The view that political concern for the common good "could not be separated" from divine commandments was the central axis of the political theology of ingression. Unjust rule on earth could not be separated from spiritual injustice, and the false doctrine of separation, marshaled to justify serfdom, was contrary to divine love and the common good. The program was the refutation of separation and the ingression of apparently disparate registers. The passage is a clear rejoinder to Luther's 1523 "On Secular Authority," which defended secular authority through the doctrine of "two realms" or "two kingdoms," taken from Augustine's division of the City of God and the City of Man. The doctrine of separation justified unconditional obedience to temporal authority in this life to ensure salvation in the next. Further, it validated political theological arguments against radical social change in the terrestrial realm. In Luther's reply to the Twelve Articles, he wrote, "The fact that the rulers are wicked and unjust does not excuse disorder and rebellion, for punishing the wicked is not the responsibility of everyone, but of the worldly rulers who bear the sword" (Baylor, *German Reformation* 109). For the peasants, Luther's logic was circular. "Wicked" rulers were responsible for "punishing the wicked." "Disorder" designated the people in struggle against a social order that expressed this infernal logic, and the political theology of ingression articulated the gestures of disordering.

In the same month that "To the Assembly of the Common Peasantry" was published, Luther penned his infamous pamphlet, "Against the Robbing and Murdering Hordes of Peasants," an invective charging that disobedience to governing authority was unchristian and "merited death in body and soul" (131). He urged the princes and lords of Germany to "smite, stab, and slay" the rebellious peasants (134). The abolition of serfdom, Luther dreaded, "would make all men equal, and in turn the spiritual kingdom of Christ into a worldly, external kingdom; and that is impossible" (112). Against Luther, "To the Assembly" theorized that the earthly realm was not distinct from the celestial: "And what about their serfdom? Damn their unchristian, heathen nature. How they torture us poor people! We are the spiritual serfs of the clergy and the bodily serfs of the secular powers" (109). The condition of serfdom was not to be "ruined in body and goods," and the peasants were subject to the "spiritual serfdom" of being forsaken in soul under the perfidious guidance of the ecclesiastical lords (120). "Spiritual serfdom" did not merely constitute the structure of the peasants' social position; it was ratified by the conscious acceptance of servility. The pamphlet warned the peasants that if they continued to labor for lords and pay them the heriot or death tax in quiescence, "you will become true slaves" (125). Spiritual and physical enslavement would end only through conscious rebellion on earth, a temporal, terrestrial revolt whose stakes were also eternal and whose field was internal (in the soul) and external (in the social). The aim and act of spiritual and material unshackling was clearly declared in the third article of the Twelve Articles: "It has hitherto been the custom for the lords to treat us as their serfs, which is pitiable since Christ has redeemed and brought us all by the shedding of his precious blood. . . . Therefore, it is demonstrated by scripture that *we are free, and we wish to be free* [*dass wir frei sind und sein wollen*]" (Scott and Scribner 254; my emphasis). The peasants' call for freedom from bondage was simultaneously a statement of theological fact. They argued that freedom, won through suffering and faith, was conferred directly on the inner worlds of the poor by God. In this view, the lower classes knew well the path of suffering that led to faith. From a modern perspective, this was the appearance of revolutionary consciousness. The statement was at once a command to destroy the social structure of serfdom and a declaration that this had already transpired in the consciousness that pushed them to assemble and rebel. In his analysis of Müntzer's theology, Hans-Jürgen Goertz suggests, "Suffering, upheaval, and a change of loyalties; what occurs in the inner space of the faithful . . . is externalized in a revolutionary change of governmental and social structures" ("Thomas Müntzer" 74). If the abolition of serfdom was, in Luther's view "impossible," the peasants understood that they themselves were the bridge between the condition of serfdom and becoming the impossible: "to be free." The ingression of the spiritual and temporal revealed that between the statement of fact, "we are free," and the demand, "we wish to be free," lay their own self-authorizing action, guided by the Holy Spirit, undertaken in the present tense.

The political theology of ingression was rooted in the belief that the Holy Spirit was a direct, moving channel from God to each person, regardless of class or nation, an idea that proved to be corrosive to the hierarchy of the Middle Ages. The view that the Holy Spirit was a pure language that knew no religious or racial boundary resounded in Müntzer's sermons: "The Christian faith which I preach [disagrees] with that of Luther, but it is identical with that in the hearts of the elect throughout the earth, Psalm 67. For even if someone were born a Turk he still has the beginning of the same faith, that is, the movement of the holy spirit" (III). Of all reformers, Müntzer was most appreciative of other faiths (Riedl 521). He praised rabbinic theologians for their exegetical concern with spiritual rather than temporal matters, studied the Qur'an, and took the radical view that "Turks, pagans, and Jews" were better suited to experience true faith than Lutherans because of the role of spirit in their faith (Müntzer 234; Riedl 521–22). The primary division, for Müntzer, was between the elect, who heeded the call of the Holy Spirit, and the godless, a term almost exclusively used for Catholic, Lutheran, and secular authority (Drummond 348). The idea that the poor laity possessed a truly divine vision of the social situation was a great inversion of the medieval social order: "For anyone who does not practice deception is regarded as a real idiot. . . . Do not let yourself be seduced by your hypocritical priests into a restraint based on counterfeit clemency and kindness. For the stone dislodged from the mountain by no human hand, is a large one now; the poor laity and the peasants have a much sharper eye for it than you" (Müntzer 245). The lucidity of the poor was a virtue of their structural position: without power or property, they were not endemically tempted by greed or pride. The political theology of ingression demanded an inversion: that the peasants turn the world "upside down" (Luther, "On Secular Authority" 14).

The ingression of the word into the deed followed from the bridging of the spiritual and temporal realms. "The interest-exacting priests," Müntzer preached, "gulp down the dead words of scripture and pour out the mere letter and the untried faith (which is not worth a louse) upon the poor, the really poor people" (367). Across Müntzer's theological writings, *dead* refers to the "vainglorious words" (202–3) that were separated from sincere experience and action. The condition of real faith held an "alien message" to the world, and the union of word and deed alone conferred holy authority (22). By this compass, it was the poor, with their experience of suffering and being "tested in crises of faith in all kinds" (200), who were close to "the living God" (200).

The union of the head and the heart was an anatomical homology of the ingression of the word and the deed that expressed a theology of nearness: "For God stands so close to you that you do not believe it" (29). The peasants' theology counseled against visions of other places or different times. Salvation is never elsewhere, never heavenward; salvation is always closer to us than we think, it is to be found where we feel. Theological writings repeatedly contrasted the view that the heart was where the Holy Spirit would come to reside, not in the church or in iconography, which drew the attention outward and upward. The clergy, in the peasants' view, obscured the radical simplicity of faith, introducing the tangled mediations of their own authority between the people's hearts and God. In his 1523 "Protestation or Proposition," Müntzer wrote, "The word, on which true faith depends, is not a hundred thousand miles from them, but they see how it springs out of the abyss of the heart" (203). Salvation was attainable only through a radical process of suffering and inner experience. The path to heaven was not a no-place, an elsewhere, or an abstraction "a hundred miles from them"; it was a path that led directly back to oneself and the "abyss of the heart" where true faith could reside. The task was to enter one's own life and body: "Every man should beat a track into his own self and then, when he is moved, realize that he himself is a holy temple 1 Cor. 3,6" (Müntzer 293). Because of the "poison of the godless" or the false teaching of the preachers, the poor mistook the doors of the church as the gateway to salvation, "hence each of them stays outside the temple, his great unbelief preventing him from entering into his own heart" (292). If "fanatic" was an epithet for the insurgent peasants, it also had its resonances, as Müntzer urged them to see themselves as a temple, or *fanum*. This leveling theology was a thunderous disruption of the theologico-political choreography of the social order, which required the intercession of clergy for access to faith and the divine. Its movement was almost perfectly perpendicular to Luther's separation of the word of God and the temporal realm.

The ingressions of the spiritual and the temporal, the head and the heart, the clergy and the laity, the word and the deed, would lead to the blending of earth with heaven. Müntzer's liturgy instructed that the Sanctus, a hymn that reads "heaven and earth" are full of divine glory, must be sung by all in order to instill in each person that "God is in him, *not imagining* or conjecturing that God is, as it were, a thousand miles away, but that the heavens and the earth are full, full of God; that the father is continually bringing the son to birth in us" (Müntzer 173; my emphasis). Müntzer bewildered the division between heaven and earth in the teaching that the proper place of the Holy Spirit was the heart. Heaven was entered, not through payment or obedience or waiting for another life, but through the voiding process of suffering. Heaven and hell were embodied, earthly states of being (*Theologia Deutsche*, ch. 11). The basic arc of this teaching was taken from the esoteric theologies of Johannes Tauler, the *Theologia Deutsche*, and Meister Eckhart, which came to Müntzer's attention through a mystic woman who served as his cook in Orlamünde (Ozment 83; Goertz, "Thomas Müntzer"; Drummond 42). Goertz argues that Müntzer's theology wed the *vita contemplativa* of mystical theology with the *vita activa* of the revolutionary task (*Innere* 15). The inner experience of suffering and despair cleared the way for the Holy Spirit, and in turn resistance in the "world" must be broken in the same way; the poor performed the same purgative function in the world that suffering had performed in their souls (145). The division of this world and the next, of heaven and earth, was an exposition of what the instructions for the Sanctus also expressed: that the theology of the Holy Spirit insisted that God could be everywhere and was most likely to enter the hearts of the poor. Thus, Müntzer wrote, "The angel declared to the mother of God: '*Nothing is impossible for God*' . . . when we come to faith: 'we must believe that we fleshly, earthly men are to become gods through Christ's becoming man' . . . *to be totally transfigured into him, so that this earthly life swings up into heaven*, Phil. 3" (279; my emphasis). As Luther wrote of "the impossible" abolition of serfdom, the political theology of ingression sung of becoming the impossible, swinging earthly life up to heaven and bringing heaven "to birth" in the body. After the abolition of serfdom, the peasants' most commonly repeated economic demand, for common access to common lands, was based on a theological vision of loving one's neighbor, selflessness, and virtue (Scott and Scribner, "Twelve Articles," "Forcheim Articles," "Stolberg Articles," "Erfurt Articles," "Confession of Hans Sippel of Vacha"). The claim to common lands was echoed across Germany. In Thuringia peasants forced the Count of Stolberg to sit on a rock outside his castle and write the following statement, which was dictated to him, promising to "make free what Christ had made free: wood, water, meadow, hunting, for each to use according to his need, wood for fuel, shelter, and building" (Scott and Scribner 201). Article 4 of the Twelve Articles states, "Until now it has been the custom that no poor man has had the authority to hunt game or fowl or to catch fish in flowing water. We think this is completely improper and unbrotherly; rather, it is selfish and not compatible with the Word of God" (Baylor, *German Reformation* 79). At first blush, the economic demand for the peasants' renewed access to privatized lands for fishing and hunting seems rather moderate in the scope of the insurrection. However, the enclosure of the commons and their transfer to private property was regarded as a theological evil. This evil could be challenged by revolutionary, collective, and divine action or, in Strauss's formulation: it could be "eradicated."

The call for common meadows and waters was radicalized in the more essential demand that echoed in 1525: *omnia sunt communia. Omnia sunt communia* was the apogee of the political theology of ingression: to put all things in common in body and goods was at once to join in a common life of spirit. The most studied expression of this demand during the Peasants' War comes from a recorded confession of Thomas Müntzer. After the last battle of the Peasants' War at Frankenhausen, Müntzer's confession, extracted and recorded by his captors, read that the goal of the uprising had been "*Omnia Sunt Communia,*" to put all things in common (Müntzer 437).[3] These aims were almost a direct quotation of Acts 2, which reads, "All who believed were together and had all things in common; And they were selling their possessions and belongings and distributing the proceeds to all, as any had need" (Acts 2:44–45).

While Müntzer's confession is the most widely studied, it was one voice in a chorus that called for "all things in common." The Allgäu Articles, written in February 1525, was one of the first oaths binding the peasants together as a band. The oath concerned "matters spiritual and temporal," which, the peasants warned, "was no carnival prank" (Scott and Scribner 127). "First," the articles of the band read, "we will stand by one another and by the holy Gospel . . . and set life and goods and all that God has given us thereto and lay down life and limb for one another" (126). The articles called for the laity's authority to control their churches and to appoint and dismiss pastors. The oath's preamble, declaring a new phase of peasant organization through a lateral, binding oath, declared a method that was at once the goal—"to set life and goods" and "life and limb" in common. The equal redistribution of goods, understood as a spiritual and temporal gesture, was an ordinary practice of peasant bands. "The Field Ordinances of the Franconian Peasantry" in April 1525 outlined formal roles chosen by election and subject to recall (supreme commander, color sergeant, captains, provost marshal, wagon master, master of the watch, master of the arsenal, kitchen supervisors, etc.). Among these was "master of the spoils," a formalized Robin Hood–like position appointed to ensure that "booty will be distributed equally" (162). This everyday practice of equal distribution during the rebellion was routinely theorized as a divine mode. In turn, the theory was a daily practice in peasant armies.

The first lines of the first oath of the Territorial Constitution of Tyrol (1526), a document written to recruit soldiers to fight for a new social order in the mountainous region where the rebellion continued after the 1525 defeat at Frankenhausen, read, "First you will swear to bring together body and goods, not to separate from one another, but to work and live with one another" (Baylor, *German Reformation* 101). The political theology of ingression literalized allegory: to "not separate" meant that the call for a common life was, simultaneously, a mandate to share goods, life, and labor. A report from the last mass peasant assembly of the rebellion in Schweinfurt on June 1, 1525, describes the thoroughgoing call for the redistribution of wealth. It reads:

> What gave [the Lords of the fortress of Würzburg] even greater dread was that the peasants [occupying Würzburg] had almost drunk up all the clergy's wine and had been heard to say publicly that since *they were supposed to be brothers with one another the same should befall everyone, and the rich should share with the poor,* especially those who had acquired it from the poor man. *The same was heard from many in the countryside,* where many a prosperous man, who had hitherto looked on and taken pleasure in the peasants' enterprise . . . began to scratch his head and reflect what a troublesome outcome and end the affair might have. (Scott and Scribner 167; my emphasis)

The generalization of the sentiment that the rich should share with the poor, especially the wealth that had been appropriated from peasant labor, had begun to ring "across the countryside" with the storm bells.

Even after the brutal defeat of the peasants, the demand-wish of *"omnia sunt communia"* had not been stamped out. It appears in the revolutionary pamphlet of Hans Hergot, a printer and colporteur, whose print shop in Nuremberg printed Luther's New Testament and Müntzer's "Manifest Exposé of False Faith." He was arrested in May 1527 for distributing "On the New Transformation of the Christian Life," whose authorship was ascribed to him. The pamphlet, likely printed earlier that spring, recounted a prophecy of a propertyless form of the world to come and reflected on the defeat of the peasants. Using the extended metaphor of a cow producing milk, Hergot laid the blame for the insurrection on "the scribes" whose false teaching led the nobility to "suck" the peasants "dry" (Baylor, *Radical Reformation* 221). Hergot described the emergence of a "new disposition of the earth," where "no one will remain in his social estate as he now is, for everybody will be integrated in a single order" (218). The prophecy begins,

> In order to promote the honor of God and the common good, I, a poor man, know those things which are in the future: that God will humble all social estates, villages, castles, ecclesiastical foundations, and cloisters. And he will institute a new way of life in which no one will say, "That is mine." . . . And everything that grows on the land belongs to the church and the people who live there. Everything is bestowed for common use, so that people will eat from one pot, drink from one vessel. . . . And the people will all work in common, each according to his talents and his capacities. And all things will be used in common, so that no one is better off than another. (211)

Hergot's Joachite prophecy foretells a time when words gain their fullest social content in spirit and act—a new disposition that would transform language. The reality of "common use," Hergot predicts, will extinguish the need for possessive pronouns. The pamphlet foretells a time when "desires for selfish gain will be done away with. And a longing for the common good will prevail over the whole village" (213). At that time, Hergot divines, the phrase often used in prayer, "'Our Father,' will be meaningful: our, our, our" (213). This prophecy, set in the future tense, was in reality backward looking. "A New Transformation" shared the themes that ran throughout the texts of the Peasants' War, but its conclusion was a defense of the peasants and an elegy for their struggle and its forms of life. The call for common property in the pamphlet resounds with the political theology of ingression—it was articulated as a desire to join divine words with practical acts, to collapse the distance between the ordinary and the eternal. The political thought of the peasants was a form of limit-thinking whose core was the gesture of uniting what had been wrongly, violently separated, to continuously thread the spirit of the common good through the latticing hands, legs, and arms of collective, fleshly life.

Conclusion

If the enterprise of political theory has been the activity of an individual reflecting on political events from the synthetic, imaginative perspective of order, the German Peasants' War presents a serious challenge to this frame. First, because the struggle was waged, articulated, and theorized by those who embodied disorder and who were pathologized as fanatics by the authorities and political thinkers like Thomas More. The basic unit and voice of the Peasants' War was collective—no clear singular author appears to reflect on the conjuncture from a detached vantage, and the individuals who have been distinguished by historians, like Thomas Müntzer, are examples of theologians who synthesized and justified collective demands that emanated from the common, embodied intellect of the masses. The political demands of this period were at once theological, existential, and economic and were expressed through a political theology of ingression, a political theology that confounded the proper role of the theorists and more fundamentally of the relation of thought and action. The Peasants' War betrays traditional political thought's constitutional inability to recognize the collective, acephalic, immanent, and insurgent theoretical forms that emanated from mass rebellion. To think with the German peasants is to be confronted with a worldview in which thinking is not separate from acting, in which theoretical forms are at once also their content, and in which theorizing is a fundamentally collective endeavor of bodies in movement. To follow peasant thought is to trace a thread of those for whom the dominant order was a crisis, and who, in response, saw their task: to become the emergency. So much has already been expressed by the peasants themselves: "We are free, and we wish to be free." To think with the peasants is to contend with the indomitable awareness that life *is* the measure of itself. ∎

O. L. Silverman is a PhD candidate in Political Science at the CUNY Graduate Center. They are currently writing a dissertation titled "Profane Heaven: Utopia, Apocalypse, and the Politics of the Imagination." They can be reached at lsilverman@gradcenter.cuny.edu.

ACKNOWLEDGMENTS

For their immense support and generous comments on drafts of this essay, I would like to thank Joe Albernaz, Robyn Marasco, Aaron Carico, Milo Ward, Alex Dubilet, Danielle Hanley, the CUNY Political Theory Workshop, the special issue editors, Max Tomba and Loren Goldman, and the editors at *History of the Present*. Thank you also to Stuart Smithers and SF friends.

NOTES

1 In regions with an established territorial state, *Landschaft* referred to the territorial diet, the state's representative assembly for various estates (clergy, nobles, townspeople, and sometimes peasants). In areas without a unified state or diet, it referred to the inhabitants of a region, either rural residents or all commoners (non-nobles). Where territorial authority was established, the *Landschaft* replaced representative assemblies, asserting power within the existing juridical framework. In areas without diets, the *Landschaft* formed a new self-governing body, as in Memmingen (Baylor, *German Reformation* 25–26).

2 Marcuse, in turn, takes the term from Whitehead, who used it for analogous, yet different purposes. For Whitehead, *ingression* describes the passage of an "object" or an eternal element of nature into the temporal realm. See *Concept of Nature* ch. 7; *Process and Reality* 23; Moore.

3 Whether these were Müntzer's words is a matter of dispute. See Scott, *Thomas Müntzer* xviii; Drummond 272.

WORKS CITED

Baylor, Michael G. *The German Reformation and the Peasants' War: A Brief History with Documents.* Boston: Bedford/St. Martin's, 2012.

Baylor, Michael G., ed. *The Radical Reformation.* Cambridge: Cambridge University Press, 1991.

Blickle, Peter. *The Revolution of 1525: The German Peasants' War from a New Perspective.* Translated by Thomas A. Brady Jr. and H. C. Erik Midelfort. Baltimore: Johns Hopkins University Press, 1985.

Bloch, Ernst. *Thomas Münzer: Als Theologe der Revolution.* Frankfurt: Suhrkamp, 1984.

Buck-Morss, Susan. *Hegel, Haiti, and Universal History.* Pittsburgh: University of Pittsburgh Press, 2009.

Colas, Dominique. *Civil Society and Fanaticism: Conjoined Histories.* Stanford, CA: Stanford University Press, 1997.

Drummond, Andrew. *The Dreadful History and Judgement of God on Thomas Müntzer: The Life and Times of an Early German Revolutionary.* New York: Verso, 2024.

Dubilet, Alex. "Insurrectionary Obscurities: On Destituent Aspects of Popular Insurgency in the Haitian Revolution." 2024. Unpublished manuscript.

Ebert, Teresa L. "Manifesto as Theory and Theory as Material Force: Toward a Red Polemic." *JAC* 23, no. 3 (2003): 553–62. https://www.jstor.org/stable/20866585.

Edwards, Mark. *Printing, Propaganda, and Martin Luther.* Minneapolis: Fortress, 2005.

Fischer, Sibylle. *Modernity Disavowed: Haiti and the Cultures of Slavery in the Age of Revolution*. Durham, NC: Duke University Press, 2004.

Goertz, Hans-Jürgen. *Innere und Äussere Ordnung in der Theologie Thomas Müntzers*. Leiden: Brill, 1967. https://doi.org/10.1163/9789004474017.

Goertz, Hans-Jürgen. "Thomas Müntzer." In *Protestants and Mysticism in Reformation Europe*, edited by Ronald K. Rittgers and Vincent Evener, 56–77. Leiden: Brill. https://doi.org/10.1163/9789004393189_005.

Goertz, Hans-Jürgen. *Thomas Müntzer: Apocalyptic, Mystic and Revolutionary*. Edited by Peter Matheson. Edinburgh: T&T Clark, 1993.

Hanley, Danielle. "Choral Inclination: Coming Together as the World Falls Apart." *Philosophia* 50, no. 5 (2022): 2551–70. https://doi.org/10.1007/s11406-022-00548-2.

James, C. L. R. *The Black Jacobins: Toussaint L'Ouverture and the San Domingo Revolution*. New York: Vintage, 1963.

Joseph, Celucien. "'The Haitian Turn': An Appraisal of Recent Literary and Historiographical Works on the Haitian Revolution." *Journal of Pan African Studies* 5, no. 6 (2012): 37–55.

Lerner, Ross. *Unknowing Fanaticism: Reformation Literatures of Self-Annihilation*. New York: Fordham University Press, 2019.

Luther, Martin. *The Ninety-Five Theses and Other Writings*. Translated by William R. Russell. New York: Penguin, 2017.

Luther, Martin. "On Secular Authority." In *Luther and Calvin on Secular Authority*, edited by Harro Höpfl, 3–19. Cambridge: Cambridge University Press, 1991.

Manuel, Frank K., and Fritzie P. Manuel. *Utopian Thought in the Western World*. Cambridge, MA: Belknap, 1979.

Marcuse, Herbert. *An Essay on Liberation*. New York: Penguin, 1973.

Moore, Duston. "Whitehead and Marcuse: The Great Refusal, Universals and Rational Critical Theories." *Journal of Classical Sociology* 7, no. 1 (2007): 83–108. https://doi.org/10.1177/1468795X07073953.

More, Thomas. *The Essential Works of Thomas More*. Edited by Gerard B. Wegemer and Stephen W. Smith. New Haven, CT: Yale University Press, 2020.

More, Thomas. *Utopia: Latin Text and an English Translation*. Cambridge: Cambridge University Press, 2006.

Müntzer, Thomas. *The Collected Works of Thomas Müntzer*. Edited and translated by Peter Matheson. Edinburgh: T & T Clark, 1994.

Nesbitt, Nick. *Universal Emancipation: The Haitian Revolution and the Radical Enlightenment*. Charlottesville: University of Virginia Press, 2008.

Ozment, Steven. *Mysticism and Dissent: Religious Ideology and Social Protest in the Sixteenth Century*. New Haven, CT: Yale University Press, 1973.

Pineda, Erin. *Seeing like an Activist: Civil Disobedience and the Civil Rights Movement*. Oxford: Oxford University Press, 2021.

Riedl, Matthias. "Gog and Magog or Allies? The Perception of the Ottoman Empire in Martin Luther and Thomas Müntzer." In *Gog and Magog: Contributions toward a World History of an Apocalyptic Motif*, edited by Georges Tamer, Andrew Mein, and Lutz Greisiger, 507–32. Berlin: De Gruyter, 2024. https://doi.org/10.1515/9783110720235-019.

Roper, Lyndal. "'The Common Man,' 'The Common Good,' 'Common Women': Gender and Meaning in the German Reformation Commune." *Social History* 12, no. 1 (1987): 1–21. https://www.jstor.org/stable/4285567.

Roper, Lyndal. "Emotions and the German Peasants' War of 1524–6." *History Workshop Journal* 92 (2021): 51–81. https://doi.org/10.1093/hwj/dbab020.

Scott, Tom. *Thomas Müntzer: Theology and Revolution in the German Reformation*. New York: Palgrave Macmillan, 2014.

Scott, Tom, and Robert Scribner, eds. *The German Peasants' War: A History in Documents*. Atlantic Highlands, NJ: Humanities Press International, 1991.

Skinner, Quentin. *Visions of Politics*. Cambridge: Cambridge University Press, 2002.

Strauss, Leo. "What Is Political Philosophy?" *Journal of Politics* 19, no. 3 (1957): 343–68. https://doi.org/10.2307/2126765.

Taubes, Jacob. *Occidental Eschatology*. Translated by David Ratmoko. Stanford, CA: Stanford University Press, 2009.

Tomba, Massimiliano. *Insurgent Universality: An Alternative Legacy of Modernity*. Oxford: Oxford University Press, 2021.

Toscano, Alberto. *Fanaticism: On the Uses of an Idea*. London: Verso, 2017.

Trouillot, Michel-Rolph. *Silencing the Past: Power and the Production of History*. Boston: Beacon, 2015.

Vázquez-Arroyo, Antonio Y. "Sheldon S. Wolin and the Historicity of Political Thought." *Good Society* 24, no. 2 (2016): 146–63. https://doi.org/10.5325/goodsociety.24.2.0146.

Whitehead, Alfred North. *The Concept of Nature: Tarner Lectures*. Cambridge: Cambridge University Press, 2015. https://doi.org/10.1017/CBO9781316286654.

Whitehead, Alfred North. *Process and Reality: An Essay in Cosmology*. Corrected ed. New York: Free Press, 1985.

Wolin, Sheldon S. *Fugitive Democracy and Other Essays*. Edited by Nicholas Xenos. Princeton, NJ: Princeton University Press, 2018.

Wolin, Sheldon S. *Politics and Vision: Continuity and Innovation in Western Political Thought*. Expanded ed. 1960; repr., Princeton, NJ: Princeton University Press, 2006.

Éric Vuillard

TRANSLATED BY MARK POLIZZOTTI

Excerpts from *The War of the Poor*

In Bohemia

And this wasn't the end of the story. It's never the end. The heart resumed beating in Bohemia; just after Wycliffe's was stilled in England, a certain Jan Hus took up his mantle and translated his *Trialogus* into Czech. And then he too began agitating. He preached in Bethlehem Chapel in Prague in favor of church reform. And off it went again: the pope issued a few more bulls that floated off toward Bohemia but snagged one by one on the little spires of Prague.

And now the pope called for a crusade against the king of Naples, and here was Jan Hus getting up on the pulpit of Bethlehem Chapel and preaching disobedience. He preached that one should love and pray even for the enemies of Christ, and thundered that true repentance could not be gained from buying indulgences, or from violent crusades, or from princely power. It was done. Again the words had been spoken: *not from money, or power, or princes.* Those same small words might change form and tone, but never their target. Each time they come back into the world, their struggle is always against money, influence, and power. Little by little, those words would become ours. They would take a long, long time to make their way to us. We still hear them, faintly, in Jan Hus's sermons, but perhaps they'd never been heard very clearly.

Then came the riots. The people rose up. Prague was in flames. The rioters were hunted down. Students burned the papal bulls, so they chopped up the students with axes. And then it all turned even uglier.

A general council was convened. At the time, three popes were laying claim to Peter's throne: the pope of Rome, the pope of Pisa, and the pope of Avignon. Gregory XII, John XXIII, and Benedict XIII. That's a lot of names and numbers to keep straight; it was complicated. And in the midst

HISTORY of the PRESENT ▪ A Journal of Critical History ▪ 15:1 ▪ April 2025
DOI: 10.1215/21599785-11561542 © 2025 Duke University Press

of this imbroglio, they fretted over Hus's body. The leading canonists knocked themselves out over it: Is Hus a heretic? Let's have a look at his liver, his gall bladder, his foreskin. Yes, he is. No doubt about it. He said the host does not become flesh. Without further ado, they summoned him to Constance; then they threw him in jail, tried him, and burned him alive. He was coifed with a cardboard miter and bound to a stake. And Jan Hus burned, he burned like wood, like straw. He burned like the heart.

■ ■ ■

It was therefore in Bohemia, in the Bohemia of Jan Hus—nearly a century afterward, but the memory of it was still vivid and ideas make their way—that Thomas Müntzer the recalcitrant arrived. For twenty-five years, the rebellious population had stood against the allied European armies; for twenty-five years they had been Hussites, Taborites, fanatics of every stripe. Eighteen thousand men had died at the Battle of Lipany. For twenty-five years, they had relegated purgatory, revoked mortal sins, renounced the monarchy for the reign of God only. They had even demanded the end of the state and the redistribution of wealth. That's where things stood.

And Thomas Müntzer, as soon as he arrived, drafted his *Prague Manifesto*. He wrote it in German and had it translated into Czech. Müntzer rejected the debates among the learned theologians; esotericism made him sick. He appealed to public opinion. It's one aspect of his greatness. The most profound theses demand to be known by everyone.

He expresses himself impulsively, in no particular order, following the burning thread of his desire. For Thomas Müntzer has one desire, and the desire that makes you a cardinal is not the same desire that makes you Thomas Müntzer. Something terrible inhabits him, agitates him. He is enraged. He wants the rulers' skins, he wants to sweep away the church, he wants to gut all those bastards. But maybe he doesn't know this yet, and for the moment he is choking it down. He wants to put an end to all that pomp and miserable circumstance. Vice and wealth devastate him; their conjunction devastates him. He wants to inspire fear. The difference between Müntzer and Hus is that Müntzer is thirsty, hungry and thirsty, terribly hungry and thirsty, and nothing can sate him, nothing can slake his thirst. He'll devour old bones, branches, stones, mud, milk, blood, fire. Everything.

The Insurgency of Ordinary Men

The Peasants' War began in Swabia, near Lake Constance. Then it spread toward the Tyrol and the north. It was a succession of revolts, not only among peasants but also in the city, among workers. Müntzer had spoken to the poor, and for a while he tried to unite the discontented masses. He ordered Count Mansfeld to "humble himself before the lowly." The count had never heard such a thing! Müntzer declared that all the birds of the sky shall devour the flesh of the princes. It's a quote from the Bible.

He signed his letters *Thomas Müntzer with the sword of Gideon*. He went off the deep end. He believed himself inspired. He was. He was inspired by green leaves, dung, smallpox, clouds, by the great hive of cities, by his ideas of liberation, by the trampled fields, by smallholdings and estates, by uprooted vines, by tariffs, by charges, by insulting nicknames, by scythes, palings, spears; yes, he was inspired by the great rictus of the ailing beast, by the torn curtain, by salvos, workshops, routine labor, and heaps of facts; yes, he was inspired by God, but God is the real scar, the commerce of waves, "a blackened bundle of frustration and torpor."

It was while trying to organize a revolt in Thuringia, in Allstedt, that Müntzer broke away from the other preachers. Things acquired an undercurrent of societal rage. The well-to-do fringe of his sympathizers started to fret. He spoke of a world without privilege, property, or government. He called Luther "the easy-living flesh of Wittenberg." He said, "All the world must suffer a big jolt." He said, "The lords themselves make the poor man their enemy. They cannot remove the cause of rebellion, so how can it turn out well in the long run? Oh, sires! How beautiful it will be to see the Lord smash down the old pots of clay with a rod of iron! That is what I say—and if that makes me a rebel, then so be it." And so it was.

■ ■ ■

On March 17, 1525, Mühlhausen rose up, mere days after Müntzer's arrival. He had not wanted this rebellion, which came too soon. But that's how facts are, they happen when they happen. Müntzer resigned himself. Since the revolt had started, he proclaimed, "Stir it up in the villages and especially among the miners and other good fellows who will be useful. We must sleep no longer." He encouraged Balthasar, Barthel Krump, Valentin, and Bischof to lead the way. The heart must become larger than all the castles, more solid than all the armor. Time to strike, while the iron is hot. "On, on, onward!" he cried. "As long as they live, it is not possible to be emptied of the fear of man. You can be told nothing about God as long as they rule over you. On, onward, while you have daylight. God marches before you, so follow, follow!"

At that point, Kurt von Tütcheroda joins him, Heinrich Hack joins him, Christoph von Altendorf joins him. And he writes letter upon letter; his is initially a war of words. Thomas Müntzer knows how to put pen to paper. There's something lively and fateful about him, an aroused hatred, a wicked turn of mind, but also gentleness. Nietzsche secretly took inspiration from him, from the Müntzeresque gush and extravagance. But Müntzer is a man of action; he gets carried along by his own prose. He does not despise the commoner, the ordinary man. Müntzer is daffodil and thistle, nettle and sap. He quotes Daniel: "Power will be given to the people." We're a long way from Nietzsche.

■ ■ ■

The revolt grinds on. In Hesse, in Upper Franconia, in Thuringia, in the Harz Mountains, in Saxony, from all corners, people are jostling, pushing, and shoving one another. Mühlhausen and Erfurt are at the heart of this popular uprising. Castles are razed, ramparts smashed; everywhere people are saying that the peasants are revolting, that they're going all the way to Rome. They say that people are rising up even on the outer fringes of Christendom, even among the Turks!

At first, the princes don't know what to do; the world seems to breathe faster, it is perpetual daylight, birds eat dirt, beasts sleep on the hoof. The Landgrave of Hesse, Philipp I the Magnanimous, is twenty years old; he is a clever lad, but self-centered and untutored. A nasty mug has young Philipp, and the very fine portrait of him from ten years later—a painting that is now in a corner of the Wartburg Museum, beneath an overly bright window—shows a bulging forehead, protruding eyes, a pained scowl, and greasy skin.

Around 1504, just as Philipp was coming into the world, but very far away from there, in Cathay, the good Shen Zhou was painting oranges and chrysanthemums. He had first painted them in his mind, petal by petal, peel by peel, quarter by quarter, pit by pit. And that day, as he was painting them on a long textile scroll, there was a light, chill wind. On November 13, 1504, his scroll of ink and pale colors folded in on itself. The birds flew off into the landscape, the solitary fisherman raised his head, the chestnuts fell into the water, the boat drifted a moment from shore. And in the tall grass sprouting among the rocks, between the dead branches, the little crab of time came to tickle the painter's fingers. Shen Zhou was old. Sitting by the river, he felt some of his sap and strength drain away from him; the disk moon sank into the pail. A few touches of gray and black were added, a leaf curled up. His training as a painter had been slow, and late in life his death would be gentle. He had painted landscapes, flowers, animals, and he passed away in a forest of saplings. At that moment, thousands of miles away, Philipp of Hesse, I mean the five-year-old who would become the Landgrave of Hesse, felt a strange shiver, like a surge of antecedence. A branch scraped the wall, the night moved. And even if you don't give a shit whether or not the Chinese painter of rocks and birds had some mysterious kinship of the soul with the Landgrave of Hesse, fantasies are nonetheless one path to the truth. History is Philomela, and they raped her, or so they say, and cut out her tongue, and she whistles at night from deep in the woods.

■ ■ ■

Faced with this upheaval, the Landgrave of Hesse didn't know what to think. He was young and impetuous. He paced round and round Luther's room, where the great man had lodged, and through the small window gazed at the rooftops of Wartburg. The sun was out. The countryside was all in green, and smoke no longer poured from the chimneys. The town was big and pretty enough, but from above, like this, that day, it seemed to him that a kind of light fog was hovering over it, a halo; he couldn't say what it was.

Still, the prince had to decide, so as not to leave Müntzer time to organize; since the month of April, he'd had an army. He had ordered expeditions throughout his territory and quashed several rebellions. On May 3, he had beaten the peasants from Fulda. Still, he hesitated. Should he march on Mühlhausen? Should he defy Müntzer?

■ ■ ■

In Mühlhausen, Müntzer was occupied with reforms; but the revolt ended in a petty democracy of artisans. His companions from Allstedt joined him, and he immediately began preaching to the weavers of Mühlhausen, the miners of Mansfeld: "Anyone who has a desire to fight against the Turk does not have far to go: he is here on our door-steps. . . . The princes' souls are in peril, for God wants them pulled out by the root!" But even that tone no longer sufficed; it didn't enflame enough people, didn't move fast enough. And so, when Müntzer learned that a crowd was rebelling in Frankenhausen, and that its numbers were swelling as the neighboring peasants poured in, he called upon the town of Sonderhausen to rise up. "Attack the eagle's nest!"

The threat became clearer; the princes banded together. The Landgrave of Hesse cut off all connection between Frankenhausen and other groups of peasants in Franconia. On March 12, 1525, Müntzer took to the roads. He had with him three hundred men, no more, like Gideon. He believed he was reenacting the fable. He was going to war, as in the Bible, praying, exulting, calling for a miracle, in an atmosphere of Doomsday.

Müntzer Beheaded

We want stories; we say they illuminate; and the truer the story, the better we like it. But no one knows how to tell true stories. And yet we're made of stories, we've been captivated by them since childhood: "Listen! Read! Look!"—our truth be done, may it draw us near and send us far with pictures and words.

∎ ∎ ∎

Concerning the end of Müntzer, there exists a legend of cowardice with many variants. Müntzer supposedly fled and hid and they found him and turned him over to Count von Mansfeld and he was imprisoned in a dungeon and tortured and supposedly he recanted and implored the princes for mercy and dictated a contrite letter to the inhabitants of Mühlhausen. I don't believe a word of it. These scurrilous legends come along to bow the heads of renegades only after they have been denied the right to speak. Their sole purpose is to make the tormenting voice sound within us, the voice of order, to which we are ultimately so attached that we surrender to its mysteries and hand it our lives.

Müntzer was married; about his wife, we know almost nothing. We know she had been a nun, then had embraced his cause, and that after the disaster, after the wooden horse and the gouging of eyes, her life was spared. They say, too, that she was pregnant at the time and that she was beaten and molested. We know of only one letter from her, a plea: "I humbly implore Your Princely Grace to please consider my great misery and poverty. I've heard it said that Your Princely Grace thought it wise for me to return to the convent. This is the favor I implore." Ernst Bloch has written that this letter is riddled with inconsistencies. Personally, I find it heartrending.

They also say that Müntzer had children. To avoid persecution, they had to change their names and adopt the diminutive Münzel, which means "small change," "alms."

∎ ∎ ∎

And now, here is Thomas Müntzer, in the same spot as his father. Surely it was terrible to find himself there at the end, chained, in the midst of a crowd. I don't know what he was thinking about. I reject doubt, treachery, renunciation. It hardly matters. Because he was so bad at hating, because he had sought the reasons for his existence so far from himself and transmuted his hatred into bitter faith, because he had so strongly felt the power of the = sign, and because one does not get bread or freedom except by grabbing it, he found himself there.

I won't delve any further into his thoughts; I leave them to him. Here he is before us, on the scaffold, a million miles from retentive pleasure. I see him. Thomas Müntzer! And he is no longer the little Thomas of before, he is no longer the street urchin of the Harz Mountains, the son of the dead man, no longer even an object of study; he is any man, any fleeting life.

He is going to die now. He is going to die. He is thirty-five. His anger brought him here. All the way here. They have mangled his body, his arms, his legs; he's bleeding. He is worn out.

Then the blade rises. Faces are there in the hundreds, all around. They watch, stunned, not sure they're seeing right. The beggars, the tanners, the reapers, the poor sods watch, they watch! And what do they see? They see a small man under a great burden. They see a man like them, his body shackled. How small a man is, how fragile and violent, inconstant and severe, energetic and full of anguish. A look. A face. Skin. Suddenly the blade falls and slices his neck. Oh! How heavy a head is, a good several pounds of bone and jelly. And how the blood spurts! His head will be impaled. His body will be dragged over the scaffold and thrown to the dogs. Youth is endless, the secret of our equality immortal, and solitude wonderful. Martyrdom is a trap for the oppressed. Only victory is desirable. I shall tell of it. ■

ACKNOWLEDGMENTS

Excerpts from Éric Vuillard, *The War of the Poor*, translated by Mark Polizzotti (New York: Other Press, 2020), pp. 27–31, 51–59, 75–59. Reprinted by permission of Other Press.

Martin Luther

TRANSLATED BY ANDREW DRUMMOND

A Letter to the Princes of Saxony, Concerning the Rebellious Spirit

June 1524

To the most illustrious high-born Princes and Lords, Lord Friedrich, Electoral Prince, and Johann, Duke of Saxony, Landgrave of Thuringia and Margrave of Meissen, my most gracious lords:

The mercy and peace of Jesus Christ our savior be with you. It has always been the misfortune of the holy word of God that, when it thrives, then Satan will strive against it with all his might. At first it will be with his fist and sacrilegious force; and when that does not succeed, then he will use false tongues with lying spirits and teachers, so that, where he cannot subdue by force, then he can oppress with trickery and lies. That is what he did in the beginning, when the Gospel first came into the world; he attacked it with force, using the Jews and heathens, and spilled much blood and made a complete martyr of Christianity. But when that did not work, he threw up false prophets and lying spirits, and filled the world with heretics and sects, until the Pope, the last and most powerful Antichrist of all, brought the whole thing crashing down with sects and heresy.

And so it has now come to pass, as we can see, that God's righteous word is being assailed as it always has been. The Pope, the emperor, kings, and princes senselessly attack it with force of arms and want to subdue, condemn, slander, and persecute it without trial or recognition. But their judgment and our defiance has long been established, Psalm 2. Why do the heathens rage and the people deceive so unprofitably? The kings of the earth revolt and the princes take counsel with each other against the Lord and his anointed. But he who resides in heaven mocks them and the Lord laughs at them, for he will speak to them in his wrath and terrify them with his anger. Certainly,

HISTORY of the PRESENT ▪ A Journal of Critical History ▪ 15:1 ▪ April 2025
DOI 10.1215/21599785-11561553 © 2025 Duke University Press

that is what will happen to our raging princes as well, and they have brought it on themselves, for they wish neither to see nor to hear: God has made them so blind and obdurate that they will run against each other and be smashed to pieces. They have been sufficiently warned.

Satan sees all this quite clearly and understands that such raging will be unable to succeed. Yes, he remarks and feels that—as is the way with God's word—the more it is repressed, the further it will go and grow. So he now begins to work with false spirits and sects. Therefore we must be alive to that and certainly not allow ourselves to be led astray. For it must be, as Paul said to the Corinthians: there must be sects so that those who are armed will be able to see them. Now when Satan had been expelled [from Zwickau], he wandered around in the desert places for one year or three, and sought a resting place but did not find one, until he settled down in Your Princely Graces' principality and made himself a nest there, from where he thought to attack us, under our shelter and protection. For in Duke Georg's principality, although it is very close by, this very terrifying and invincible spirit (as he boasts) pretended to be so good and mild that no bold signs of courage or defiance could be proven. But he also cried out horribly and complained that he had to suffer greatly, so that no one up until then dared touch him with fist or words or quill pens, and he invented a great cross on which he suffered. Satan, however carelessly and causelessly he might lie, just cannot hide himself.

Now I find it a particular joy that it was not our people who began this sort of thing. And they boast themselves that they are not of the same opinions as us, they neither learned nor received anything from us. But they say they come from heaven and hear God himself speak with them, as if they were angels, and it is a bad thing that Wittenberg teaches faith and love and the cross of Christ. You must (they say) hear God's voice yourself, and suffer God's work within you, and feel how heavy your burden is. The Scripture means nothing, yes, Bible, babel, babble, etc.[1] If we were to talk about them with such words, then their cross and their suffering would (I believe) become even more cherished than Christ's suffering, and they would value it even higher—that is how much the poor spirit boasts about his suffering and his cross. And they are not prepared to accept the slightest doubt or objection to their heavenly voices and God's work, but rather they just want to be believed straightaway as an authority, without considering that I have neither read nor heard this arrogant, proud holy spirit (if that is what he was).

But this is neither the time nor the place to make a judgment of their teaching, for I have already done that twice. But if it is important, then by God's grace I will judge it again. I have written this letter to Your Princely Graces for this reason only, that I have understood from their writings that this same spirit does not simply want to stick to words alone, but wants to threaten with his fist and set up a power against secular authority and straightaway start a worldly rebellion. Satan never lets the rascal be seen, for that would be to give too much away. What might the spirit unleash if he wins the support of the common people? I have indeed heard from this same spirit here in Wittenberg that he considered it necessary to complete the task with the sword. I thought then that they will end up attacking secular authority and make themselves the lords of the world. But Christ replied to Pilate, denying that very thing and said that his kingdom was not of this world, and even the disciples taught that they should not become like worldly princes.

Although I expect that Your Princely Graces will know better than I can advise you how to deal with this, it is nevertheless my duty to apply my submissive energies to make a contribution, and I ask Your Princely Graces most humbly to take a serious view of this, and from your responsibility and duty to exercise reasonable force to defend yourselves against such mischief and prevent rebellion. For Your Princely Graces know well that your power and worldly sovereignty are given to you by God with the command that they should be used to keep the peace and punish the unruly, as St. Paul taught in Romans 13. So Your Princely Graces should neither slumber nor miss this opportunity. God will demand an answer of you if you neglect to use the sword that has solemnly been entrusted to you. And the people and the world would not forgive it if Your Princely Graces were to tolerate and suffer such rebellious and outrageous violence.

But even if they claim (as they are wont to do with splendid words) that the spirit drives them, and that they must take action and exert force, then I would reply: firstly that it must really be an evil spirit that bears no fruit other than the destruction of churches and monasteries and the burning of holy statues. The worst knaves in the world can achieve the same thing, especially when they feel safe and meet no resistance. But I should be more worried if the Allstedt Spirit were to come to Dresden or Berlin or Ingolstadt, and rage and destroy the monasteries there and burn the icons there. Secondly, the fact that they boast of having the spirit means nothing, for we have here the words of St. John: "you should test their spirits beforehand, whether they come from God." But this spirit has not yet been put to the test, but simply proceeds with violence and unrest as he pleases. If it was a good spirit, then he would allow it to be tested beforehand and humbly submit to judgment, as Christ did.

One test of the good fruit of the spirit would be that it did not creep into corners and hide from the light, but rather had to stand openly before enemies and opponents and answer questions. But the Allstedt Spirit avoids this, as the Devil avoids the cross, and all the while holds forth from his nest with the most disgraceful words, just as if he had been filled with the holy trinity. Now this blatant bragging really shows what kind of spirit he is. For he boasts in his writings that he would willingly stand before an impartial gathering, but would not stand and answer in a corner with two or three people; and yet he freely offers his body and soul etc.

Could someone tell me: who is this courageous and spiteful spirit who hems himself in and is unwilling to stand before an impartial gathering? And why will he not answer questions in the company of two or three men? What kind of spirit is that who fears two or three people and cannot tolerate an impartial audience? I will tell you: he smells the roast. Once or twice he fell on his nose in my monastery at Wittenberg, and that is why he fears the soup, and that is why he will not stand up unless the audience is his and they agree with his excellent words. If I (who have absolutely no spirit and cannot hear the heavenly voices) had said anything of the sort to my Papists, how they would have cried out loud and stopped up my mouth.

I cannot boast with such lofty words, nor can I stand defiant. I am but a poor, miserable man and have not ordered my affairs skillfully from the beginning, but only after great shaking and fear (as St. Paul also admits of himself, 1 Corinthians 3—although he did indeed say that he knew of the voice of God). How humbly I attacked the Pope at first, how I begged, how I sought answers, as my first writings have shown. Nevertheless, with my poor spirit, I managed to do something that this gobbler of worlds has not attempted; he, rather, ducks and dodges in a most knightly and manly fashion, and even boasts of all this dodging as if he possessed a knightly, elevated spirit.

I stood at Leipzig in order to dispute in front of a most dangerous audience. At Augsburg, I appeared unaccompanied before my greatest enemy. At Worms I stood before the emperor and all his noblemen, although I well knew that my escort had been held back and that all manner of wild strange perfidy and spite was aimed at me. How weak and poor I was then, but my heart was bold at that time. If I had known that as many devils had taken aim at me as there are roof tiles in Worms, then I would still have ridden into that town; and yet I had none of those heavenly voices, and none of God's talents and works that we have been hearing about from the Allstedt Spirit. And yes, I have sat in corners with two or three people, just who and where and how they wanted. My stupid, poor spirit had to stand as free as a flower in the meadow, with neither time, nor person, nor place, nor manner nor many voices, but had to be ready and willing to stand before anyone to give answer, as St. Peter teaches.

And this spirit which flies as high above us as the sun above the earth, which can hardly see us little worms down here, agrees with various harmless, friendly, unreliable judgments and listeners, and does not wish to give answers to two or three people in a room apart. He feels something that he does not like feeling, and hopes to terrify us with mighty great words. Let him try: we can only do what Christ gives us to do; if he abandons us, then we will be terrified by a rustling blade of grass. But if he wishes to hold us close, then the spirit of his great name will pass into us. And if Your Princely Graces will permit me, it is now necessary to reveal what passed between me and this spirit in my rooms, so that Your Princely Graces and all the world will know and understand that this spirit is certainly a lying devil and yet a pathetic devil. I have always had such a one annoying me, and still have one today. For the spirits who go around with proud words and thump the barrel, they do nothing; but those who creep secretly will do mischief before one even hears them.

I have had to say all this so that Your Princely Graces do not shy away from this spirit, nor delay in dealing with it, but that they seriously issue orders to prevent violence and avoid the destruction of your monasteries and the burning of your holy images. You must tell this spirit to behave as he should, and test him beforehand to determine whether he is for us or for the Papists. For they think (God be praised) that we are worse enemies than the Papists, even though they make use of our victories to the full, take wives, and abandon Papal laws that they have never questioned, without once risking their necks. I, on the contrary, have succeeded so far by risking my body and my life. I must boast of this just as St. Paul did, although it is a madness, and I would rather not do so, if it were not for the lying spirits.

They say repeatedly that their spirit is too high and our spirit is too low, and their things cannot be recognized by us; to this I reply that St. Peter also knew quite well that his spirit, and that of all Christians, was higher than that of the heathens and Jews, but yet he asked that we should always be ready and willing to answer everyone mildly. Christ also knew that his spirit was higher than that of the Jews, but he lowered himself and took the opportunity that was offered and said: who among you accuses me of a sin? If I have spoken evil of Annas, then tell me so etc. I know, too, and am certain of it through God's grace, I who am more learned in the scriptures than all sophists and Papists. But God has so far mercifully protected me from arrogance and would continue to protect me if I were to refuse to give answer to, or be heard by, the least Jew or heathen or anyone else.

And why do they put their thoughts in print, if they are not prepared to stand before two or three, or before an impartial gathering? Or do they think that their writings are suited for some unimportant impartial gathering, but not for two or three? Yes, I am astonished that they have so completely forgotten their spirit and now want to teach people both in speech and in writing, if at the same time they boast that everyone should hear God's voice for himself; and mock us because we spread God's word both in speech and in writing, as if that had no value; and they have a much more delightful church service than even the apostles and prophets and Christ themselves, all those who spread God's word both in speech and in writing, and never once said anything about the heavenly voice of God that we must all hear. Thus this humbug performs so many tricks that he can no longer understand what he says.

But I know that we, who know the Gospel, understand whether we are poor sinners with the correct spirit, or—as St. Paul says—*primitias spiritus*, the first fruits of the spirit, or whether we do not yet have the fullness of the spirit. That is none other than the same single spirit that distributes its gifts most wonderfully. We already know what faith and love and the cross are, and there is no more elevated knowledge on earth than of faith and love. That is why we can both know and judge whether a teaching is true or false, in accordance with faith or not; and therefore how we know and judge this lying spirit. He wants to set aside the scripture and the spoken word of God, and root out the sacraments of baptism and communion, and drag us into the "spirit," so that we may seek God with our own actions and free will, and so wait upon his works, and set limits to the time and manner of his actions upon us. Such dreadful presumption is set out in their writings, where they write with express words against the gospel of St. Mark, namely, that St. Mark incorrectly wrote about baptism in his last chapter. But they do not smack St. John in the mouth quite as badly as they do St. Mark. He who is not otherwise born of water and of the spirit, John 3 etc., they point at the word *water* and ignore it and so completely reject bodily baptism in water.

But I would really like to know, since the spirit is not without fruit and their spirit is so much worthier than ours, whether it also bears better fruits than ours? Yes, it really must bear better fruits than ours, for it is worthier and higher. So we teach and confess that our spirit, which we preach and teach, will yield the fruits of St. Paul, in Galatians 5 where he talks of love, joy, peace, patience, goodness, faithfulness, mildness, and moderation. And he says in Romans 8 that he kills the work of the flesh and with Christ crucifies the old Adam together with all its lusts, Galatians 5. In summary, the fruits of our spirit are the realization of the ten commandments of God. Now the Allstedt Spirit, who does not accept our spirit as his, must come up with something better than love and faith, peace, patience, etc. Since St. Paul said that love was the greatest fruit, 1 Corinthians 13, he must therefore do something even better than God commanded. I should really like to know what that would be, especially as we know that the spirit is attained through Christ alone, so that we might obey God's command, as Paul says in Romans 8.

But if they try saying that they do not live as they teach, and do not possess such a spirit that will yield such fruits, then I could understand them saying that, for one could easily comprehend that that is not a good spirit which speaks through them. We readily concede, although it is not necessary to understand this by means of heavenly voices and higher spirits, that we sadly do not do everything as we should. Yes, St. Paul in Galatians 5 states that nothing can be done while spirit and flesh sit side by side in this world and are in conflict. So I do not think there is anything special about the fruit of the Allstedt Spirit, except that he wants to strike out with his fist and break down timber and stone; until now, they have shown no signs of love, peace, patience, goodness, and mildness, so that the fruits of this spirit are not too common. I, however, can demonstrate many fruits of the spirit in God's grace with our people, and could easily set my person, which is the least and most sinful, against all the fruits ever produced by the Allstedt Spirit, however much he reproaches my life.

But when someone reproaches someone's teaching on account of a fragile life, then that is not the work of the holy spirit. For the holy spirit reproaches false teaching, and has patience with the faith and the life of the weak, as Paul teaches in Romans 14 and 15 and in many other places. I am not troubled because the Allstedt Spirit is so barren, but only because he denies everything and wants to establish different teachings. I would have had just as little with which to challenge the Papists if they had only taught correctly, for their wicked lives did not do much damage. But because this spirit wishes to go further, and get annoyed at our wretched lives, and make insolent judgments of our teaching because of the teacher's life, then he has amply proven what he is. For the spirit of Christ judges no one who teaches correctly and is patient and supports and helps those who do not yet lead a good life, and so it does not despise the poor sinners as our pharisaical spirit does.

Now all this affects the teaching, as will be shown in due course. So we arrive at a conclusion, most honorable sirs: that Your Princely Graces should not forbid the words of the preaching. Just let them preach confidently and briskly whatever they want and against whomsoever they want. For, as I have said, there must be sects, and the word of God must march out into the field and fight, which is why the Evangelists were called a mighty host,

Psalm 67 [68], and Christ was seen as a king at the head of his army by the prophets. If their spirit is correct, then he will not fear us and will stand firm. If ours is correct, then he will have nothing to fear from us. One can let these spirits square up to each other and exchange blows. If some people are misled by them, so be it: that is the cost of war. Wherever there is conflict and battle, then some must fall and be wounded. But he who fights justly will be crowned.

But if they want to do more than merely fight with words, if they want to destroy and strike with the fist, then Your Princely Graces should intervene: it is either us or them. They should straightaway be banished from the land and warned not to return. We are quite prepared to allow and tolerate it if you fight back with words, so that the true teaching is protected. But we declare that you should not use force or mobilize any troops. For we, who champion God's word, should never fight back with the fist. This is a spiritual struggle that will win hearts and souls from the devil. And it was written by Daniel that the Antichrist should be destroyed without human hand. It is also written in Isaiah II that Christ in his kingdom will fight with the spirit of his mouth and punish with the rod of his lips. Our task is to preach and to suffer, and not to lash out with fists or defend ourselves. Christ and his apostles never knocked down any churches or chopped up any pictures, but rather won over hearts with the word of God: and then the churches and pictures fell down of themselves.

This is how we should act. Firstly, we should wrest hearts away from monasteries and spirits. When this has been done, then churches and monasteries will lie waste and the land-owning lords can do what they want with them. For what interest do we have in timber and stone when we have once saved the hearts that lived inside them? Look how I have conducted myself: I have never once touched a single stone and certainly never damaged or burned a monastery. And yet, as a result of my words, monasteries and nunneries in many places now lie empty, even in those areas with princes who are opposed to the gospel. If I had attacked them with violence, like those prophets, then the hearts would have remained in captivity all over the world, and I would never have affected either timber or stone in a single place. And what use would that have been? Fame and honor may have been achieved in this way, but the salvation of the soul would certainly not have been. Some people consider that I have done more damage to the Pope without using any violence than some mighty king might have done. But because these prophets are pleased to do something remarkable and better, and still do not succeed, they leave these souls standing hopeless, and instead attack timber and stone—that is the new and wonderful work of the higher spirit.

But they may want to object and say that the law of Moses permits the Jews to destroy all graven images and uproot the idolatrous altars. Answer: they know themselves quite well that God has done much work since the beginning, either through his own words and faith or through many saints. And the epistle to the Hebrews sets it out quite clearly and says that we should follow the example of the beliefs of those saints, since we cannot emulate the actions of all those saints. If the Jews cast down the altars and idols, then at that time they had the commandment of God to do so, which is something we do not have in our times. For when Abraham offered his son as sacrifice, he had God's clear commandment to do so; but anyone who later sacrificed their children in emulation did not act righteously. It is not right just to emulate those acts—or else we should have ourselves circumcised and do all manner of Jewish things.

Yes, if it was right that we Christians should destroy churches and rage like the Jews, then it would follow that we have to physically kill all non-Christians, just as the Jews were commanded to slay the Canaanites and Amorites as well as destroy their idols. In this way, the Allstedt Spirit would accomplish nothing other than bloodshed, and those who did not hear his heavenly word would have to be strangled so that the people of God did not have to put up with such offenses, which are after all so much greater in living non-Christians than in wooden or stone images. That was the commandment that was given to the Jews as the people who were protected by God's miracles—and to be sure they were God's people; and yet they carried this out with orderly force and leadership, and not in a disorderly horde. But this spirit has not proved with any kind of miracle that he is of God's people, and he stirs up trouble all on his own as if he alone were God's people, and proceeds without any orderly force sanctioned by God, and wishes people to believe in his spirit.

Trouble must be put aside through the word of God, for although all visible trouble must be destroyed and done away with, it is of no use if hearts are not thereby brought from faithlessness to the correct belief. For a faithless heart will always find new trouble for itself, as also happened among the Jews when they set up ten idols where before they had destroyed only one. That is why the New Testament explains the correct way of driving out the devil and all his trouble: that is, by using the word of God to turn hearts away, by which means the devil and all his pomp and power will fall away.

Here I will leave this affair, and beg Your Princely Graces most submissively to deal very severely with this raging fanaticism, so that God's word alone is discussed in this matter, as befits Christians; and to prevent rebellion for which Everyman seems to be too much inclined. For those are not

Christians who wish to use their fists over and above words, and are not at all prepared to suffer when they think they are full to overflowing with ten holy spirits.

May Your Princely Graces be forever fortified and protected by God's mercy. ■

1　　In German: "Bibel, Babel, Bubel." Luther chooses here to partially quote a phrase of Müntzer's, in his "Prague Manifesto" of 1521, where he contrasted "Bible and Babel." Luther's word "Bubel" does not exist but sounds like the German word for knave— "Bube." Other translations offer themselves, including "rabble" (from knavery) and "bogle" (an evil spirit or goblin), and a couple of less polite words beginning with "B." But I suspect Luther was simply aiming for dismissive alliteration: hence "babble."

TRANSLATED BY ANDREW DRUMMOND

The Twelve Articles of the Peasantry

The Fundamental and Just Articles of All the Peasantry
and Tenants of the Spiritual and Temporal Lords,
by Whom They Consider Themselves Oppressed

March 1525

To the Christian reader be God's peace and grace through Christ.[1]

There are many enemies of Christ who have now taken the occasion of the gathering of the peasants to slander the gospel, saying: Is this the fruit of the new gospel? To be obedient to none, to rise up in many places and band together in great numbers and in great force to conspire to reform the spiritual and temporal powers, to uproot them, yes, even perhaps to murder them? These articles which follow are the answer to all these godless and blasphemous critics, firstly so that they cease their mockery of God's word, and secondly so that we can justify in a Christian manner the disobedience, yes, the rebellion of all the peasants. Firstly, the gospel is not a cause of rebellions or insurrections because it speaks of Christ, the promised Messiah, whose words and life taught nothing more than love, peace, patience, and unity, so that all who believe in this Christ should be loving, peaceful, patient, and united. This is the basis for all the articles of the peasantry (as will clearly be seen)— to hear the gospel, and to live according to its message. How, then, can the enemies of Christ call this a cause of rebellion and disobedience? Some enemies of Christ are opponents of the gospel, who set themselves up and conspire against its demands and requirements—but this is not caused by the gospel, but rather by the devil, the most harmful enemy of the gospel who stirs up such feelings in his supporters through a lack of faith, in order that the word of God (which teaches love, peace, and unity) should be suppressed

HISTORY of the PRESENT ▪ A Journal of Critical History ▪ 15:1 ▪ April 2025
DOI: 10.1215/21599785-11561564 © 2025 Duke University Press

and removed altogether. Secondly, then, it follows that the peasants who use this teaching and guidance in their articles cannot be called disobedient or rebellious. For if God wishes to hear the peasants (who are anxiously calling to live according to his word), then who dares to obstruct the will of God? Who dares to intervene in his judgment? Yes, who dares to strive against his majesty? Did he not hear the children of Israel calling out to him, and did he not deliver them from the hand of Pharaoh, and can he not save his people even today? Yes, he will save them! And not too long from now! So, Christian reader, read these articles with great care and make your own judgment.

The articles now follow.

The First Article

Firstly, it is our humble plea and request, and the wish and opinion of all, that from this time on a community should have the power and authority to choose and appoint our own pastors. And that we should also have the authority to remove the same pastor if he should behave improperly. This same appointed pastor should preach us the holy gospel loud and clear without adding any human teachings or laws, for constantly imparting to us the true belief will give us cause to ask God for his mercy, and instill and confirm in us the true belief. For if his grace is not instilled within us, then we will always remain just flesh and blood, which is of no use, as it clearly states in the scripture that we can only come to God through the true belief and can only be saved by his mercy. So such a guide and pastor is necessary for us. And this demand is based on the scriptures.

The Second Article

Secondly, although the just tithe is set out in law in the Old Testament and is confirmed in the New, nevertheless we wish to pay a just tithe in corn, but only where it is warranted: since the tithe should be given to God, and shared with his servants, then the pastor who clearly preaches God's word deserves to receive it. From now on, we wish that this tithe should be collected and brought in by church wardens, and our pastor, appointed by the whole community, should take from it what is sufficient for himself and his dependents, after the whole community has agreed on it; and anything that is left over should be distributed to the needy poor who live in the same village, according to their need and with the consent of the whole community; and anything that is left over after that should be stored, in case there is a need to travel for the defense of the country—in this way, there would be no need to impose a land tax upon the poor people, for the costs could be met from this reserve. And if it happened that one or more villages were forced to sell off the rights to the tithe in some emergency, then those who can prove that they purchased it with the consent of the whole village need not be expropriated; instead, we wish to reach fair agreements with them, according to circumstances, and to redeem the tithe in installments. But if the purchasers did not buy it from any village, and their forefathers just took it for themselves, then we do not wish and are not obliged and do not intend to pay them any more, regardless of whether they are clergymen or laymen, except as mentioned before for the support of our appointed pastor, and we will keep the rest back, or give it to the needy poor, as the holy scripture commands. And we will not pay the small tithe at all, for the Lord God created cattle free for Man's use; we consider it to be an unjust tithe which has been invented by men. Therefore we will not pay it any more.

The Third Article

Thirdly, it has been the custom until now for lords to treat us as their own property. This is something to be deplored, since Christ redeemed us all by shedding his precious blood, regardless of whether it is a lowly shepherd or the highest in the land, with no exceptions. So the scripture proves that we are, and wish to be, free. It is not the case that we will be completely free and have no authority over us, that is not what God teaches us. We should live according to the commandments, not according to the free lusting of the flesh; we should love God and see him as our Lord in our neighbor, and do everything that God commanded us to do when he spoke at the Last Supper. Therefore we should live according to his commandment. But does this commandment teach us that we should not be obedient to our lords? No, we should obey not just our lords, but we should humble ourselves before everyone. So we will freely obey our elected and lawful ruler (set over us by God) in all proper and Christian matters; and we have no doubt that you, as true and righteous Christians, will release us from our bondage or else prove to us from the scriptures that we belong to you.

The Fourth Article

Fourthly, it has been the custom until now that no poor man should have the right to catch wild game, wild fowl, or fish in running water, which we consider to be quite improper and unbrotherly, and selfish and quite contrary to the word of God. And in some places the lords maintain the wild game to our harm and great loss, for we must suffer while the dumb animals gobble up our crops (although God created them for Man's use), and we must keep quiet about it, which is an offense against God and against neighbors. When the Lord God created Man, he gave him power over all animals, and over the birds in the air and over the fish in the water. So it is our request that if someone owns a stretch of water, then he will have to prove with written evidence that he bought the water by consent. If he can prove this, then we do not wish to take it from him by force, but we want to consider the matter in a Christian manner, and in the spirit of brotherly love; but anyone who cannot provide sufficient evidence should then hand it back to the community, just as it is.

The Fifth Article

Fifthly, we have a grievance about the cutting of wood, for our lordships have taken all the woods to themselves, and when a poor man needs some, then he has to purchase it at double the price. It is therefore our opinion that those woods which have not been purchased, whether they are owned by clergymen or laymen, should be passed back to the community again, and the community should have the authority to allow anyone to freely take all that he needs for firewood, and also what he needs for building, also free, provided it is taken with the knowledge of someone who has been appointed by the whole community. If there is evidence that the woods have been purchased, then we should negotiate about their use in a brotherly and Christian manner. But if the woods were simply taken and afterward sold to someone else, then we should reach an agreement that is formed by brotherly love and the holy scripture.

The Sixth Article

Sixthly, we have a heavy burden of providing labor, which is increased day by day and daily grows more frequent. We request that this be done more considerately and that we are not burdened so much, but rather that we should be allowed, as our fathers did, to provide labor only according to the word of God.

The Seventh Article

Seventhly, in future we do not wish to allow the lords to lay burdens on us, but rather a lord will allow land to be held in a proper manner, by an agreement between the lord and the peasant. The lord should no longer force or oblige the peasant to undertake labor without pay. In this way, the peasant can use and enjoy his holding without being burdened. But if the lord feels that the labor is necessary, then the peasant should willingly obey his lord before any others: however, he will do it on a day and at a time that is not to the peasant's disadvantage, and it should be for a just wage.

The Eighth Article

Eighthly, we have a grievance that many of us who hold land are obliged to pay rent that is greater than the yield of the land. The peasants then lose their property and are ruined. In this case the lords should let honorable men inspect these holdings and agree on a fair rent, so that the peasant does not have to work for nothing. For every laborer is worthy of his hire.

The Ninth Article

Ninthly, we have a grievance about serious crimes, for people are constantly making up new laws and we are not being punished according to the seriousness of the crime but rather sometimes according to great envy and sometimes according to favoritism. It is our opinion that punishments should be carried out according to the old written laws and taking into account the circumstances, and not according to whim.

The Tenth Article

Tenthly, we have a grievance that some people have taken for themselves the same fields that once belonged to a community. We will take these back into the ownership of our communities, unless they have been properly purchased. But if they have been improperly purchased, then a friendly and brotherly agreement should be reached, according to the circumstances.

The Eleventh Article

Eleventhly, we wish to completely abolish the custom known as "heriot" or death tax. We cannot suffer or permit a man's widow and orphans should be shamefully robbed against God and honor, which is happening in many places (in all kinds of ways). The very people who should protect and defend them are instead fleecing and skinning us. If they had had the least excuse for it, then they would take everything. God will no longer tolerate this, but will be rid of it completely. In future, no man should be obliged to pay this tax, whatever it amounts to.

The Twelfth Article

Twelfthly, it is our decision and final opinion that if any one or more of these articles set out here does not agree with the word of God—which we doubt— then we will abandon these same articles if anyone can show us that they do not agree with God's word, by referring us to the holy scriptures. And if any article is conceded and is later found to be unjust, then they shall be

considered null and void from that moment on. Likewise, if any more grievances should be discovered that are based upon truth and the Scriptures and
relate to offences against God or our neighbor, we reserve the right to present
these also, and to live our lives according to the full Christian teaching and
usage. And so we beseech the Lord our God that he alone will give us this.
The peace of Christ be with us all. ∎

NOTE

1   These demands appeared in March of 1525 and in the following few weeks were
     printed at least twenty-five times in different locations. The likely author of these
     demands is Sebastian Lotzer, and they are representative of many similar sets of
     "Articles" that emerged at that time. It is clear that they reflected the main concerns
     of most of the peasant troops in southwest Germany. In the printed editions, the
     margins are cluttered with references to chapters of the Bible, each reference pro-
     viding scriptural justification for the demands.

Thomas Müntzer

TRANSLATED BY ANDREW DRUMMOND

Letter Written to Allstedt, Written from Mühlhausen, April 26 or 27, 1525

This letter was written by Müntzer, in an attempt to persuade his former parishioners in Allstedt to join in the broader Thuringian uprising. The handwritten original has not been preserved, although contemporary handwritten copies exist. It was printed by Martin Luther as part of his pamphlet *Eyn Schrecklich geschicht . . . Thomas Müntzer*, which appeared in late May 1525, and ran to at least four editions that year, with many more in the years to come.

May the pure fear of God be with you, dear brothers. How much longer will you sleep, how much longer will you resist God's Will because you think He has forsaken you? Oh, how often have I told you how it must be: God cannot reveal himself unless you stand in tranquility. If you do not do so, then your sacrifice, your heart-saddening suffering of the heart, is all in vain: you will have to start all over again and recommence your suffering. I tell you: if you are not willing to suffer for the sake of God, then you will become martyrs of the Devil. So take good care, do not be so downcast or neglectful, and stop flattering those perverted fantasists, those godless evildoers, but rather begin now and fight the Lord's fight! It is high time, make sure all your brothers do not mock God's testimony, or else they will be lost. The whole German, French, and Italian lands[1] are up in arms, the master will have his game, the evildoers will have to take care. In Fulda in Easter week, four abbeys were laid waste, the peasants of Klettgau and Hegau in the Black Forest have risen, three times one thousand strong,[2] and the army is growing ever greater. My only worry is that the foolish people will accept some false peace treaty, because they cannot recognize the harm that could be done.

HISTORY of the PRESENT ▪ A Journal of Critical History ▪ 15:1 ▪ April 2025
DOI: 10.1215/21599785-11719522 © 2025 Duke University Press

Even if there are only three of you who stand tranquil in God and seek only his name and honor, then you will not fear a hundred thousand. So: on, on, onward! It is time, the evildoers are running scared like dogs. Alert your brothers so that they may be at peace and give testimony of their change of heart. It is utterly and completely necessary. On, on, onward! Do not show pity, even though Esau comes to you speaking with kind words, Genesis 33. Take no heed of the cries of the godless, for they will come to you amicably, entreating, whining and begging like children. Do not let yourselves show pity, as God commanded us through Moses, Deuteronomy 7 (and he has revealed these things to us as well). Stir it up in the villages and especially among the miners and other good fellows who will be useful. We must sleep no longer.

Look, just as I was writing these words, a messenger came to me from Salza, saying that the people there wanted to lay hands on the administrator of Duke Georg[3] because he had secretly wanted to kill three of them. The peasants of the Eichsfeld have taken hostile action against their Junkers and wish to show them no mercy. There are many things like that which should give you an idea what to do. You must set to it, onward, for it is time. Balthasar and Barthel Krump, Valentin and Bischoff all lead the way in the dance.[4] Get this letter out to the miners. I have been told that my printer is expected here in the next few days.[5] There is nothing else I can do just now, otherwise I should really want to instruct the brothers so thoroughly that their hearts would grow far bigger than all the castles and defenses on earth belonging to the godless evildoers.

On, on, onward, for the fire is hot! Do not let your sword grow cold,[6] do not let it hang loose in your hands! Smite cling clang on the anvil of Nimrod; cast down their towers! As long as they live, it is not possible to be emptied of the fear of man. You can be told nothing about God as long as they rule over you. On, onward, while you have daylight. God marches before you, so follow, follow! The story is already written in Matthew 24, Ezekiel 34, Daniel 7, Ezra 16, Revelations 6, and all these are explained in Romans 15.

So do not let yourself be daunted. God is with you, as is written in 2 Chronicles 20, where God says, "You should not be afraid. You should not shrink back from this great host, for it is not your fight but the Lord's. It is not you who fight, so stand firm like men. You will behold the help of God." When Jehoshaphat heard these words, he fell to the ground. Thus must you also, with the help of God who will strengthen you in the true belief without the fear of Man. Amen.

Written at Mühlhausen in 1525.

Thomas Müntzer, a servant of God against the godless. ∎

ACKNOWLEDGMENTS

Original German text available in *Thomas-Müntzer-Ausgabe: Kritische Gesamtausgabe, 2, Briefwechsel*, edited by S. Bräuer and M. Kobuch (Leipzig: Verlag der Sächsischen Akademie der Wissenschaften, 2010), 403–15.

NOTES

1   "Das gantze deutzsche, frantzosisch und welsch land"—*welsch* refers generally to Italian Switzerland. But there were no peasant uprisings outside German territory at this time.

2   In Martin Luther's pamphlet *A Terrible History and Judgement of God on Thomas Müntzer* (*Eyn Schrecklich geschicht* . . .), this phrase about the number of peasants in arms was here multiplied to "three times one hundred thousand"; the actual number may have been around one hundred thousand (see Luther 362–74).

3   Sittich von Berlepsch.

4   Bartel Krumpfe, Bartel Zimmermann, Valentin Krumpe—in his "Confession" of May 1525, these people are mentioned as the ringleaders of the Allstedt League. Bischoff was a preacher in the small nearby town of Wolferode.

5   This could possibly be the man who had printed Müntzer's Allstedt pamphlets, Nikolaus Widemar. But that is by no means certain. The printer probably did arrive in Mühlhausen, but he never printed anything.

6   Luther's reprint of the handwritten letter adds "with blood" after "grow cold."

WORK CITED

Luther, Martin. *Martin Luthers Werke: Kritische Gesamtausgabe*. Vol. 18. Weimar, Germany: Hermann Böhlaus Nachfolger, 1908.

Keep up to date on new scholarship

Issue alerts are a great way to stay current on all the cutting-edge scholarship from your favorite Duke University Press journals. This free service delivers tables of contents directly to your inbox, informing you of the latest groundbreaking work as soon as it is published.

To sign up for issue alerts:

1. Visit **dukeu.press/register** and register for an account. You do not need to provide a customer number.

2. After registering, visit **dukeu.press/alerts**.

3. Go to "Latest Issue Alerts" and click on "Add Alerts."

4. Select as many publications as you would like from the pop-up window and click "Add Alerts."